THE**GOOD**FIGHT

THEGOODFIGHT
Prophetic Processing Workbook

DANMCCOLLAM

"To the victor go the spoils."

Table of Contents

Acknowledgments

When you live in prophetic community, it's difficult to know where other people's contributions leave off and where your own begin. Ultimately, our own voice is the culmination of our influences plus our innovations. I am indebted to many voices from the prophetic community which have inspired me to fight the Good Fight. I wish to acknowledge them here.

- To those who have served on The Mission leadership team over the years teaching us the value and methods of prophetic processing: Dena McClure, Keith Ferrante, Gary and Karissa Hopkins, and, of course, our fearless leaders, David and Deborah Crone. I have learned so much from doing life with you.

- To our current prophetic processing trainers at The Mission: Josh and Cherie Cawley and Bethany Hicks. Your friendship and teamwork have put the sense of family in our prophetic company.

- To our prophetic coaches who have served so many hungry hearts in prophetic processing sessions. You are the foundation of encouragement and strength upon which we build.

- To my lovely wife, Regina, who formats and processes the grammar and punctuation of all my ramblings. You are a rare and precious treasure.

- To Byron and Crystal Easterling who did the first processing of my own personal prophetic words. You two started me down this path of being a doer not just a hearer of the prophetic. I'm indebted to your wisdom and your example.

- To Graham Cooke who borrowed the words from 1 Timothy 1:18 to title our processing sessions "The Good Fight" and gave us so many helpful insights on how to process our words. May God bless your path of equipping and training.

- To Joyce Milton, who is an amazing prophetic trainer with the most creative ideas for how to capture our identity statements. Love and thanks for your out-of-the-box thinking.

I love you all and live with thankfulness in my heart for you. I wouldn't be fighting the Good Fight without your contributions in my life.

Foreword

'm convinced that the greatest pleasure of the Lord is to be believed and that He is looking for people who will partner with Him to bring His promises to fruition. This was not always my stance.

"If someone gives you a 'personal prophetic word,'" the instructor stated, "thank them for their effort, and put the word on the shelf. If it comes true, you will know it is from God." In other words, take it lightly and forget about it. This was the safe way we handled what should have been a powerful weapon of our spiritual warfare. The tragedy of this kind of response is that we never receive the transformational benefit resident in the word.

Having been raised in, educated by, and dedicated to thirty-plus years of service to what I now refer to as a "non-prophet" organization, this kind of wait-and-see response was the usual when I asked a teacher, pastor, or friend about personal prophecy. It sounded quite reasonable to me since at that time, we didn't acknowledge the New Testament office of prophet nor did we embrace those who were considered prophetic or spiritually intuitive. We thought these prophetic types were rather peculiar, and we were sure—even absolutely convinced—that God was not peculiar.

My wife Deborah and I had lived in a safe and practical world filled with family and friends, thinking it encompassed all there was to the Kingdom of God. We enjoyed the belief that God was predictable, our doctrine was sure, our values were in place, and our interpretation of Scripture was unquestionable. We were convinced that the spiritual place we were in was the best. Though down deep in our hearts, we suspected that there could be—maybe even should be—more.

THE GOOD FIGHT

I don't know if it was simply God answering the cry of our hearts or that He just got tired of hearing me misrepresent Him and His church. What I do know is that He chose to rock our world by inviting us onto a path where we could explore who He really is and how His Kingdom really works. Our acceptance to His invitation not only transformed our own lives but the entire church community we are thankful to be a part of at The Mission.

One aspect of the Kingdom Holy Spirit opened to us early on in our exploration of this invitation was the experience of prophetic culture. One of the men who has been key in helping us understand and grow in this great gift of the Spirit is the author of this ground-breaking workbook, Dan McCollam. Over the years, growing in understanding from our previous position of "If someone gives you a 'personal prophetic word,' shelve it" to living in what has become a healthy, authentic, and Bible-based prophetic culture has been the result of many people investing in our lives and the life of the church. Dan and his wife Regina, however, have been the most significant for they have been our friends and colleagues along the entire journey.

It is through Dan's teaching and ministry that we have come to know the difference between loving prophecy and fully embracing the word of the Lord. It has taken us as a couple and our congregation as a church from being awed by an accurate personal prophecy to being warriors ready to partner with God to make that word a reality.

Having our prophetic words become effective weapons was boldly illustrated to us when we were building the church sanctuary at The Mission. We had determined to build debt-free and had received numerous prophetic words declaring the provision needed as well as foretelling the power our testimony concerning the building would release. Through many miraculous provisions, we completed the building up to the point of installing the sheetrock on the walls. It was then that we realized we did not have the funds to finish the project. In fact, we were 1.1 million dollars short of the needed money. At this point, the truth of God's word to us became a weapon against the facts of our situation.

On the Monday evening of the week we would have to shut down the project, Holy Spirit provoked me to act. I picked up our prophetic weapons, which were our prophetic words, and invited Deborah, and my son, Jeremy, to accompany me to the construction site of our uncompleted sanctuary shell. It was dark, and no electricity was available, so we carried flashlights as Deb and Jeremy climbed onto the piles of sheetrock stacked around the floor. I climbed the stairs to the room designated for the video suite where I could overlook the sanctuary. We then began to declare every promise, prophetic word, and Scripture that we had been given during the building process. We did this for about fifteen minutes, felt the peace and pleasure of God, and went back home.

Foreword

There is much to the story, but let me cut to the result of those fifteen minutes of fighting the Good Fight in accordance with the prophecies previously made concerning us. The next day I shared the problem of our financial lack with a man who had already been very generous toward the building project. To my surprise, the man responded, "Well, that's interesting. I've put aside $800,000.00 in an account for you just in case you needed it. Tomorrow I will transfer it to the church so you can keep building." A month later, the remaining $400,000.00 was raised in one Sunday morning service, and the project was completed!

We have learned that what we don't fully embrace, we trivialize. And what we trivialize, we don't fully possess. As you begin *The Good Fight: Prophetic Processing Workbook*, know you are looking at a clear roadmap for the true adventurer to possess the land of their prophetic promises and win the day in the Good Fight.

—David Crone
Senior Leader at The Mission, Vacaville, CA
Author of *The Power of Your Life Message, Prisoner of Hope, Declarations That Empower Us,* and *Decisions That Define Us*

This command I entrust to
you, Timothy, my son . . .
fight the good fight.

Introduction

Timothy was perhaps the closest thing Apostle Paul had to a son. The book of Proverbs tells us that words of instruction between a father and son are a special source of wisdom and understanding. That is why Paul's instructions to Timothy about fighting the Good Fight are so very important. We need to read this not as another sermon or church instruction but as the impassioned transfer of instruction and wisdom from a father to his son. We find this fatherly wisdom in First Timothy:

> This command I entrust to you, Timothy, my son, in accordance with the prophecies previously made concerning you, that by them you fight the good fight.

1:18, NASB

For years after coming into an awakening of the gift of prophecy, I treasured prophetic words that were spoken over me and my family. However, I never really fought with or strategized with them. The prevalent teaching at the time told us to set prophetic words aside and wait to see if they come true. It was some twenty-five years later through the service and equipping of other prophets that my own prophetic words moved off of the back shelf to a biblical and strategic position. Now prophetic processing is one of the primary values of our prophetic company at my home church.

Once they have been judged, prophetic words are meant to be tools for successful warfare. The Greek word used in the above verse for "fight" is *strateuo*. It means "to make a military expedition, to lead soldiers to war or to battle, to do military duty, be on active service."[1]

---

[1] *Strong's Greek Lexicon* (KJV) online at blueletterbible.org: G4754, *"strateuō"*.

In this workbook, you will learn the tools that my prophetic company and I have utilized over the last decade and a half for fighting the Good Fight through analyzing and strategizing with our prophetic words. In the activation sections of this book, you will be asked to read over your prophetic words multiple times. Each time you read, you will discover something new about warring with those words. Don't let the repetition bog you down.

At the end of the processing workbook, you will have advanced in several, if not all, of these goals:

- Discover who you are as a new creation in Christ Jesus.
- Stand on what God has promised that He will do for you.
- Know what you can do to agree, align, and appropriate God's intentions towards you.
- Identify mindsets, cautions, and actions that will accelerate the fulfillment of promises.
- Possess a clearer understanding of your assigned spheres of influence.
- Properly discern your times and seasons to stay in rest and strength.
- Unpack the deeper meanings behind symbols, types, and metaphors.
- Identify major and minor themes in order to properly align with God's priorities for you.

The chapters in this book will alternate between those that help you discover truths and treasures in your prophetic words and those that instruct you how to war with this information. I have provided three sample prophetic words that were spoken over my life for you to practice on. You will also find additional processing worksheets in the Appendices along with a Processing Quick Reference Sheet to help you remember the steps in prophetic processing.

I believe Jesus Christ is the pattern for everything pertaining to abundant life. Regarding prophecy, we know that Jesus' life fulfilled every prophetic word ever written about Him. Scripture often records that He did specific actions in order to "fulfill what was spoken through the prophets."[2] The value that Jesus placed on fulfilling His prophetic words gives me confidence for my own Good Fight.

In Scripture, we also observe Jesus warring with His prophetic words. At the temptation of Christ, the devil challenged Jesus' prophetic identity with the words:

If you are the Son of God, tell these stones to become bread.

Matthew 4:3

---

[2] See Matt 8:17; 12:17; 21:4.

Introduction

Jesus answered from the confidence of what the Father had audibly spoken over Him at His recent baptism.

> *Man shall not live on bread alone, but on every word that comes from the mouth of God.*

v 4

This is the Good Fight of Jesus Christ. He was in essence saying, "I don't have to prove anything to you, devil. My Father said that I am His Beloved Son in whom He is well pleased." The audible voice of God is a type of prophetic word, and Jesus warred with what had been spoken over Him. The life of Christ confirms the power and value of fighting the Good Fight with our prophetic words.

Once they have been judged, prophetic words are meant to be tools for successful warfare.

I've seen this value in my own life. Now that my prophetic words have been judged and moved from the back shelf to the forefront, I war with them on a regular basis. Whenever my identity or my situation does not line up with what God has said about me, I challenge that reality with "every word that comes from the mouth of God." Positioning myself like Jesus did with what God has said about me gives me courage and confidence to stand, wait, and watch to see God do what He said He would do. As demonstrated by the life of my Savior, Jesus Christ, I have found that fighting the Good Fight with the prophetic words spoken over me is a key to abundant living. It is a fulfillment of the Lord's Prayer:

> *Your kingdom come, your will be done, on earth as it is in heaven.*

Matthew 6:10

My hope and prayer for *The Good Fight: Prophetic Processing Workbook* is that you will find a sweeter place of abundant living in Christ Jesus. I believe you will find a fresh honor for prophetic words that will attract an even deeper level of prophetic revelation. You will increase your dialogue and friendship with Holy Spirit, and you will be able to resist the challenges and temptations of the enemy. As a warrior, you will even see an acceleration of previously dormant prophetic promises.

It's time for the sons and daughters of God to arise and fight the Good Fight according to the prophetic words spoken over them.

Judging prophecy should be done in the
context of a loving community.

1

JUDGING**PROPHECY**

Growing up in a church that didn't pursue the supernatural, I really didn't even know what prophecy was. All I knew about prophecy was that my mom had a friend who married the wrong guy because of a prophetic word. The marriage ended in a tragic divorce, and the woman lived the rest of her life alone because someone had given an incorrect word. The unspoken moral of the story was clear: Stay away from prophecy; it's dangerous.

Yet, Scripture clearly disagrees with this conclusion. Paul instructed the Corinthian church:

Therefore, my brothers and sisters, be eager to prophesy, and do not forbid speaking in tongues. But everything should be done in a fitting and orderly way.

1 Corinthians 14:39-40

Again, in Paul's closing thoughts to the Thessalonian church, he said:

Do not quench the Spirit. Do not treat prophecies with contempt but test them all; hold on to what is good, reject every kind of evil.

1 Thessalonians 5:19-22

THE GOOD FIGHT

Scripture tells us that prophecy is good and that protocols are necessary.

The Word of God gives more instructions to the receiver of prophecy than to the giver.

False prophecies and lack of prophetic protocol certainly are dangerous for the Body of Christ, but a greater error may be to dispose of the prophetic altogether. Many churches have either forbidden, ignored, or so limited prophetic expression that they are quenching or suppressing the voice of the Spirit.

The Word of God gives more instructions to the receiver of prophecy than to the giver. In the above verse, God instructs that we "test them all; hold on to what is good, reject every kind of evil." Those are instructions to the prophetic receiver not limitations on the one prophesying.

I like what my friend Kris Vallotton says about prophetic ministry. Kris explains that there are two powerful people in any prophetic exchange: one is the giver and the other the receiver. The giver has the power to share what he or she believes the Lord is saying; the receiver has the power to "flush." That's right. Flush like a toilet. Everyone has the power and responsibility to test for what is good or genuine in any prophecy. Therefore, no one has to be affected by a bad prophetic word. A false prophecy should not curse or confuse anyone because we have permission to hold on to what is good and flush the rest.

The responsibility to judge prophecy is one of the foundation stones for healthy supernatural cultures. Here are four simple criteria for judging prophetic words.

1. Test the word.

Does anything in your prophetic word conflict with Scripture or the character and nature of God?

> *Do not quench the Spirit. Do not treat prophecies with contempt but test them all; hold on to what is good, reject every kind of evil.*
>
> 1 Thessalonians 5:19-22

"Test" here is the Greek word *dokimazō,* which means, "to test, examine, prove, scrutinize (to see whether a thing is genuine or not), as metals; to recognize the genuine after examination, to approve, deem worthy."[3] In order to judge whether money is counterfeit or not, experts compare it to the genuine. In testing prophecy, the genuine is always the Word of God. You can confidently "flush" anything that doesn't align with God's Word or the character and nature of God (i.e., His love, joy, peace, patience, kindness, goodness, etc.).

Yet, even in a "bad word" there may be good or accurate portions. That's why Scripture tells us to test it all and hold on to the part that is good.

Every prophetic word should pass a love test as well.

> *If I have the gift of prophecy and can fathom all mysteries and all knowledge, and if I have a faith that can move mountains, but do not have love, I am nothing.*
>
> 1 Corinthians 13:2

There are fifteen characteristics of love mentioned in 1 Corinthians 13:4-8. Among them are "love does not dishonor others" and "love does not keep a record of wrongs." If the word feels dishonoring or embarrassing or brings up past failures in a shameful way, then it probably is not wrapped in love.

Every prophetic word should pass a love test.

2. Test the source.

Does the one delivering the word have anything to gain or personally benefit from the potential outcome of the prophetic word? If a person has a self-interest in the outcome of a prophetic word, then it is difficult to know whether it has been delivered in love. No matter how impressive or well-credentialed the person giving a prophetic word is, if the word is delivered from any motive other than love, then it is not to be considered.

> *Love is not self-seeking.*
>
> 1 Corinthians 13:5

Scripture also describes the difference between heavenly and earthly wisdom in the book of James. We see in this passage how wisdom judges both the person who is delivering the word and the word itself.

---

[3] *Strong's Greek Lexicon* (KJV) online at blueleterbible.org: G1381, "*dokimazō*".

Who is wise and understanding among you? Let him show by good conduct that his works are done in the meekness of wisdom. But if you have bitter envy and self-seeking in your hearts, do not boast and lie against the truth. This wisdom does not descend from above, but is earthly, sensual, demonic. For where envy and self-seeking exist, confusion and every evil thing are there. But the wisdom that is from above is first pure, then peaceable, gentle, willing to yield, full of mercy and good fruits, without partiality and without hypocrisy. Now the fruit of righteousness is sown in peace by those who make peace.

James 3:13-18, NKJV

We see from this passage that a person who is self-seeking, bitter, or envious cannot deliver a word from above. A person cannot show partiality or hypocrisy and deliver a pure word of wisdom. A heavenly source of wisdom gives a word in meekness with the goal of peace. Consider the source. How the word was delivered and from whom does make a difference.

3. Test the effect.

Does the word resonate with you? Does it encourage, comfort, or strengthen you even if parts of the word are challenging?

But the one who prophesies speaks to people for their strengthening, encouraging and comfort.

1 Corinthians 14:3

When we ask if a word resonates with you, we are asking, "Does it produce peace, gentleness, mercy, and good fruit?"

Let's go back to the passage we examined from the book of James in point two about heavenly wisdom. James told us that earthly wisdom causes confusion and invites evil; but the wisdom from above is peaceable, gentle, willing to yield, full of mercy and good fruits, without partiality or hypocrisy. When we ask if a word resonates with you, we are asking, "Does it produce peace, gentleness, mercy, and good fruit?" Words can frighten you because they are big or far from your current reality, but they should not haunt you with dread and fear or open the door to evil.

What effect does the word have on you? Is it going against your own will? Does it violate your sense of peace or pull you in a direction that feels farther from God, your church community, or your family? There are times when a calling will require you to launch out from your current community or circumstances (like Abraham in Genesis 12:1), but you should never do so lightly or without sober and significant consideration.

4. Test in community.

Share your word with loved ones and leaders around you. How do they view the word? Are there any parts of the word they are questioning the validity of?

Scripture tells us:

> *Two or three prophets should speak, and the others should weigh carefully what is said.*

1 Corinthians 14:29

Judging prophecy should be done in the context of a loving community. Scripture tells us that we "know in part and prophesy in part."[4] Community provides healthy and broad perspective on the interpretation and application of prophecy.

Our primary text for prophetic processing talks about fighting the Good Fight through our prophetic words. Prophetic processing is warfare. The book of Proverbs gives us many instructions concerning the connection between community and waging war:

> *For lack of guidance a nation falls, but victory is won through many advisors.*[5]
>
> *Plans are established by seeking advice; so if you wage war, obtain guidance.*[6]
>
> *Surely you need guidance to wage war, and victory is won through many advisers.*[7]

You can clearly see from these passages the wisdom of judging prophecy and fighting the Good Fight with prophetic words in the context of community. Invite others you trust into the processing process.

---

[4] See 1 Cor 13:9.
[5] Prov 11:14.
[6] 20:18.
[7] 24:6.

"PREPARING FOR PROPHETIC PROCESSING" EXERCISE

The following chapters of this book will take you through the steps of analyzing and processing prophetic words you have received. Throughout these instructions, I will be using some of my own personal words to illustrate the principles taught and for you to practice the assignments on. However, there are a few things for you to do in preparation before we get started in order to get the most out of this process.

STEP ONE:

Transcribe your prophetic words to prepare for processing. Type out your words using a large font with double line spacing so you will have plenty of room for notes. At the top of each page, reference who delivered the word, where it was delivered, and the date it was delivered. For example:

John Smith to Dan McCollam
at Really Inspirational Conference
My Town, CA
March 17, 2017

STEP TWO:

Judge your prophetic words as described earlier in this chapter before beginning this process. You are free to cross out, discard, or flush any words that don't fit the criteria we talked about. Process only what is good and only what resonates in your spirit as a true word from God.

Here is a brief review of our judging criteria.

- Does anything in your prophetic words conflict with Scripture or the character and nature of God?

- Does the one delivering the word have anything to gain or any personal benefit from the potential outcome of the prophetic word?

- Does the word resonate with you? Is there a sense of internal agreement even if parts of the word challenge you?

- How do loved ones and leaders around you view this word? Are there any parts of the word that make them question its validity?

STEP THREE:

Take two or three prophetic words you have judged to be "God words" for this season and print them out on paper for easier processing.

NOTES

_____

_____

_____

_____

_____

_____

_____

_____

_____

_____

_____

_____

The truest thing in the universe about
you is whatever God says about you.

2

PROCESSING**IDENTITY**

Gideon is a Bible character with whom many of us can relate. We first meet Gideon hiding in a winepress, threshing out some wheat. He was hiding because every time it seemed like he and his family would get a little bit ahead, what they had was stolen away. Gideon worked and lived frustrated, wondering where God was. That's the situation and mindset Gideon lived under when the angel of the Lord appeared with this strange greeting:

The LORD is with you, mighty warrior.

Judges 6:12

Gideon's reality was so far from his destiny that he answered the angel in frustration,

"Pardon me, my lord," Gideon replied, "but if the LORD is with us, why has all this happened to us? Where are all his wonders that our ancestors told us about when they said, 'Did not the LORD bring us up out of Egypt?' But now the LORD has abandoned us and given us into the hand of Midian."

v 14

The angel simply answered:

Go in the strength that you have and save Israel out of Midian's hand. Am I not sending you?[8]

Now, Gideon is really challenged. He says to the angel:

"Pardon me, my lord," Gideon replied, "but how can I save Israel? My clan is the weakest in Manasseh, and I am the least in my family."[9]

Gideon had the same problem that most of us have when challenged with doing something great for God. He had already externally and internally defined himself. Our external definitions are based on

- What we do (our present performance),
- What we have done (our past, especially our failures), and
- How other people see us (the opinions of others).

In America, we often introduce ourselves to others by our external definitions:

Gideon had the same problem that most of us have when challenged with doing something great for God. He had already externally and internally defined himself.

"Hello, I'm Fred. I am a teacher."

"Hello, I'm Nancy. I am a lawyer."

We allow what we do, as well as what we have or have not done, define who we are and what we can do. This is a huge mistake. Gideon measured himself by these external markers when he said, "My family is unimpressive, and I am the least in my family."

Internal markers can be just as deceptive. When Moses was called by God to deliver a nation he said:

Pardon your servant, Lord. I have never been eloquent, neither in the past nor since you have spoken to your servant. I am slow of speech and tongue.

Exodus 4:10

That was Moses' internal definition of himself, but Acts records the truth about him:

[8] Judg 6:14.
[9] v 15.

At that time Moses was born, and he was no ordinary child. For three months he was cared for by his family. When he was placed outside, Pharaoh's daughter took him and brought him up as her own son. Moses was educated in all the wisdom of the Egyptians and was powerful in speech and action.

Acts 7:20-22

Moses' internal evaluation did not line up with reality. He was the only one in his generation without a slave mentality. Moses may have been the only one in his nation with an education, which at the time was the finest education available in the world. The young prince was considered powerful in speech and actions. Our internal definers are often marred by our own fears and failures; they do not provide an accurate view of who we truly are.

Our internal definers are often marred by our own fears and failures; they do not provide an accurate view of who we truly are.

The key to breakthrough in identity is to be eternally defined rather than externally or internally defined. Who does heaven say that you are? In Gideon's case, the angel of the Lord called him a mighty warrior. Now according to earthly and external definitions, you could only be called a mighty warrior if you were great with weapons and had won significant battles. But heaven does not operate on earthly systems. In heaven, you win battles *because* the Lord says you are a mighty warrior. The truest thing in the universe about you is whatever God says about you. In the earthly system, you are named after what you do or accomplish; in the heavenly system, you do and accomplish out of who God says you are. From heaven's perspective, the identity of the person comes first—Gideon was known as a warrior before he won a battle. Then the action—the winning of the battle, in Gideon's case—is the reasonable result of a God-given identity. Rather than your actions defining who you are; who you are defines what you can do.

This principle illustrates why prophecy is so important. It also demonstrates the difference between Scripture and prophecy. The Bible unveils who we are corporately as sons and daughters of God. We discover in the Bible virtues and qualities that all sons and daughters of God possess together. We are all priests and kings; we are all salt and light to the world; we are all the temple of the Holy Spirit. Prophecy, when it is properly judged, discloses who we are as individuals. Gideon was called to be a warrior and deliverer; Abraham was called to be a father to nations; David was a king after God's heart. Both our corporate identity revealed in the Word and our personal identity revealed through prophetic words are very important.

We must understand that we are new creations as a result of the work of Christ's redemption. This new creation identity as son or daughter of God contains an entirely different capacity for virtue and greatness than a mere servant of God. The nature of God within us releases the possibilities of heaven through us. Prophecy reveals the specializations each of us possess as sons and daughters of the King of kings. It's as though the Bible reveals my surname, and prophecy reveals my given name. The surname is something that all the children of the Father carry; the given name speaks to the uniqueness of the child. Prophecy in this way is a revelation of our heavenly identity.

Prophecy speaks from our heavenly position. Scripture tells us that we are seated in heavenly places in Christ Jesus.[10] Prophecy is so much more than information about what you could or should do. Perhaps prophecy is like overhearing how you are already known in heavenly places. It is your personal and unique revelation as one who is seated in heavenly places in Christ. When the angel approached Gideon, he addressed him as one who was already a mighty warrior. Could it be that this is how Gideon was already known in heaven? The angel of the Lord revealed a heavenly identity. Our heavenly identity reveals how we can live more abundantly and powerfully on the earth. We must learn to live from an eternal definition concerning our identity.

> **The key to breakthrough in identity is to be eternally defined rather than externally or internally defined. Who does heaven say that you are?**

All of this begs the question, "How can I know my heavenly identity?" One of the primary sources for discovering our heavenly or eternal identity is found by extracting identity phrases and descriptions from your prophetic words. Look for words that describe who God says you are. Pay attention to things or persons He compares you to. Abraham's word of prophecy revealed him as an exalted father, a father of nations, and a source of blessing. Beyond the promise of having a son, his heavenly identity was revealed through these statements. His self-view was upgraded to match God's view of him. Gideon's prophetic word from the angel of the Lord called him a mighty warrior, a deliverer of Israel, one who is strong. The prophet Samuel's prophetic act over David defined him as the next king of Israel. Later prophets defined him as a man after God's own heart. All of these examples of identity phrases extracted from biblical prophecies redefined how each of these individuals saw themselves.

---

[10] Eph 2:6.

"PROCESSING IDENTITY" SAMPLE FOR PRACTICE

Let's put this idea to practice. Three sample personal prophetic words are provided for your practice. We will use these same three prophecies in each assignment throughout this workbook. Answer keys are provided in Appendix IV for you to refer to if you are feeling uncertain. After practicing with the text provided, you will repeat the exercises in order to process your prophetic identity using your own typed out personal words.

STEP ONE:

Look for and circle statements of identity in the words below. See the examples of identity phrases I have circled in the first two paragraphs of the sample word, then proceed on to circle the rest of the identity words you find in this sample.

Sample One

Lord, I bless Your minstrel prophet in the name of Jesus, who will be used—has been used and will be used—in an international manner to help restore the tribe of Asaph in the earth. I bless him in the name of the Lord.

We are all general practitioners, but God gives us specialty grace. I acknowledge that the Lord has set you into the Body as one of the Asaphs that raises up the prophetic Levitical priests to set them in divine order so as to call forth a new sound.

And as the new sound comes forth, heaven responds to the sound of earth. When heaven responds to the sound of earth, heaven comes down and joins in the sound of earth. Then it becomes not only our praises ascending, but heaven has just descended into the earth realm.

So you are called as a culture creator and an atmospheric changer to help restore the Asaph priesthood of prophetic order in Jesus' name. Amen.

Now see if you can find any identity statements in Sample Two.

Sample Two

Last night I was praying for you, Dano, and the Lord told me that you are no longer going to be known as the town drunk. Because you've gone through a season of being foolish for God, now you are going to confound the wise.

And yeah, a change in season—literally with your identity—there is a piece of your identity that you are leaving, and you are coming into a wise thing. I saw the Lord put a helmet on your head, and it said "wisdom" across the top of it. I feel like there is incredible strategic wisdom for the nations.

I feel like you are no longer going to be known for the foolishness—and I mean the foolishness we have when we follow God—but you are going to be known for your wisdom. So you have to take off that first season that the Lord had you in and put this one on. In Jesus' name. Amen.

Don't be alarmed if you didn't find any direct statements of identity in Sample Two. We will address that in the next step.

STEP TWO:

Often identity language is implied rather than directly stated. Sample Two contains implied rather than direct statements of identity.

Examples of implied identity in Sample Two:

- "Now you are going to confound the wise."
- "You are coming into a wise thing."
- "I saw the Lord put a helmet on your head, and it said 'wisdom' across the top of it. I feel like there is incredible strategic wisdom for the nations."

Based on all the phrases about wisdom in this word, you could conclude an implied statement of identity as "a man of wisdom for the nations."

Now look for implied statements of identity in Sample Three and circle them.

Sample Three

Hundreds of thousands of dollars. Hundreds of thousands of dollars. Hundreds of thousands of dollars. Hundreds of thousands of dollars. The Lord says, too, that music companies and music stores are going to give you instruments. Music stores are going to give you instruments.

The Lord says that which you are birthing of worship in the earth will be the leading edge of an evangelistic move in the countries that you are working in. You will see your sons filling stadiums. Filling them. Filling them. Filling them. You are already starting to see it. Filling stadiums. For the Lord says it is going to increase because there is a quickening spirit upon you.

The Lord says of that which He has birthed in you, He says breathe on your sons even as Jesus breathed on his disciples and sent them. Breathe on your sons. Breathe on them. Because there is a quickening spirit. And the Lord says they don't have to know everything you know for there is a quickening spirit upon them because God is saying that they have to be accelerated. You see that in the spirit yourself. You see it in the spirit yourself.

For the Lord says there are more nations in His heart for you than what you are seeing right now. More nations in His heart for you. He is going to give you sons. I can see right now a dozen nations that God has given you sons in.

He says hundreds of thousands of dollars are going to come to you. He says ask Me. Ask Me. Ask Me for property; the answer is "yes." Ask Me for recording studios; the answer is "yes" because your sons will become fathers themselves in the anointing that God has given you.

The Lord says that He gives you a quickening spirit. The reason He wants you to breathe on your sons is so that they can go back and become fathers right quick because this is a move that is going to gather pace. It's going to gather pace. Gather pace. It is going to be like a rock rolling down a hill. It is going to go fast. It is going to go fast. So the Lord says great favor is in front of you. A huge wide open space is in front of you. Explore it!

THE GOOD FIGHT

STEP THREE:

Make a bullet list of identity statements you highlighted from the sample words, both directly stated and implied.

- Minstrel prophet
- Culture creator
- A man of wisdom
- _____
- _____
- _____
- _____

STEP FOUR:

Piece together identity words and phrases to create a personal "I Am" statement. Throughout this workbook, "I Am" statement and "identity" statement are terms used interchangeably. Below I started the sample identity statement for you. Using the remaining words from the list you created, craft an "I Am" statement revealing how the recipient of these sample words is known and seen in heaven.

I am a minstrel prophet restoring the Asaph priesthood in the earth. I am a culture creator and an atmospheric changer.

I am . . .

_____

_____

_____

_____

_____

_____

"PROCESSING IDENTITY" WORKSHEET

Gather two to three of your typed out and printed personal prophetic words. Choose words that resonate with you and which you have already judged as good and from the Lord.

STEP ONE:

Carefully read through your personal prophetic words and circle any obvious statements of identity.

STEP TWO:

Read through your words again, this time circling any implied statements of identity.

STEP THREE:

Make a list of identity statements revealed in Steps One and Two.

- _____
- _____
- _____
- _____
- _____
- _____

STEP FOUR:

Craft an "I Am . . ." statement of three to five sentences summarizing the highlights of how you are known and seen in heaven.

I am _____

I am _____

I am _____

I am _____

I am _____

NOTES

_____

_____

_____

_____

_____

_____

_____

_____

_____

_____

_____

_____

_____

_____

_____

_____

Heavenly identity can give you authority, favor, and influence beyond your current circumstance or position.

3

WARRING WITH IDENTITY

The revelation of your heavenly identity is a place from where you can fight the Good Fight. My "I Am" statement forms the standard to where I call myself up. Whenever I am about to speak and feel weak, unqualified, or unable to be powerful, I remind myself of what God has said, "You are a culture creator; an atmosphere changer." I clothe myself with these words like putting on armor and step out into the authority and favor they represent.

I believe this is what young David did in the valley of Elah in the classic Bible story of David and the giant warrior, Goliath. David had previously been anointed king of Israel through a prophetic act performed by the prophet Samuel. However, at the time, he was still only known as a shepherd boy and the younger brother to three of King Saul's warriors. David was sent by his father to the battle lines to check on his brothers and deliver food provisions to them and their commander. When David arrived at the battlefield, he heard the daily taunt of the giant Goliath defying God and the army of Israel. This mockery filled David with a righteous indignation. In contrast, Saul, the current king of Israel, had lost his confidence to connect with God because of his disobedience to the Lord and because he had built an altar to his own honor. This lost connection affected his ability to identify with and act in the manner of a king.

David went among the troops and began to ask what would be done for the man who took out this threat to Israel. The answer returned, "He would be given the king's daughter as a wife." Marrying the king's daughter would put David in alignment with fulfilling the word of the Lord. David may have also reasoned to himself, "I'm not king yet as is my destiny, so nothing bad can happen to me. This giant can't take me out." These two ideas—that he might marry the king's daughter and that he may be somewhat invincible until the fulfillment of his becoming king—may have given David extra confidence.

Notice the difference between the current king and David who carried the prophetic word of becoming king. Saul is described in Scripture as a powerful man who was a head taller than anyone else in his nation. He was arguably the biggest, baddest dude in Israel at the time. But again, Saul had lost sight of his calling as king through disobedience and compromise. David was just a shepherd boy with no reputation as a warrior, but he called on the power of his prophetic identity to act confidently in the face of a hugely intimidating foe and against overwhelming odds. This reveals one of the ways that we fight the Good Fight—we pull on the confidence and authority of our heavenly identity.

Fast-forward a few years. David has become famous for taking out the giant and delivering Israel. Saul is bitter because he sees that the favor of God and of the people has already transferred to David. David is driven out of the courts of the king and forced to hide out in a desert cave. What does the young champion do at this point? Without money, he builds one of the greatest armies in Israel's history. Without prior warfare training, he defends and expands Israel's territory. Without national resources, he defeats Israel's most powerful enemies. David did everything a king is supposed to do without a throne or position. Saul had a throne and a crown but had lost the inner confidence as king. Heavenly identity can give you authority, favor, and influence beyond your current circumstance or position.

> **Alignment is the process of simply acting like the real you.**

I've met so many people through the years who were waiting for a position to release their anointing or authority. Someone says, "I feel called to preach, but the pastor doesn't see it. He won't give me the pulpit to preach." Just like you don't need a throne to serve people like a king, you don't need a pulpit to fulfill the call of a preacher. Go out into the forest and preach to the trees; preach to your cat or dog; preach to anyone who will listen. When I heard the call to vocational ministry, no one wanted me to come preach. No one had even heard of me. I was complaining to the Lord one day, and He asked me, "What would you preach if you were invited to today?"

That question challenged me. I had been wrestling with the emotions of the call but not engaging in the preparations for such a call. I sat down that very day and wrote a sermon as if I had to preach it that night. The next day I did the same thing and every day following for one year. On the 365th day, the phone rang. I received my first invitation to preach, and I've never lacked opportunity to speak in the last thirty years.

My history is not the prophet of my future; my heavenly identity is.

You may not have a vocational ministry call, but the same rings true for those with heart dreams in any field. If the Lord says that one day you will own your own restaurant, it may not be time to run out and purchase one, but you could work in one. Learn behind the scenes. Serve well. Watch what is done and consider what could be done better. Prepare yourself for what is in your heart. Train for where you want to reign.

The following are three keys I have found for warring with your prophetic identity.

1. Agreement

The first stage of anything in the Kingdom is believing. Read through your prophetic identity statement and meditate on what it says. Practice believing that who God says you are is really true. This is your heavenly persona. This is your new creation. This is what you look like seated in heavenly places in Christ Jesus. Read your identity statement over yourself out loud and often. Embrace every word as true. Hear in your spirit the voice of God speaking this over you. Think deeply within your heart and mind that this is the truest thing about you in the universe.

2. Alignment

Alignment is defined in the dictionary as "arranging things in correct positions for agreement and alliance." In terms of your heavenly identity, alignment is simply defined as positioning yourself to agree and ally with what God says about you. It's taking off anything that doesn't look like the person heaven describes and putting on the things that do. I like how Paul said it:

> *Get rid of the old yeast, so that you may be a new unleavened batch—as you really are . . .*

1 Corinthians 5:7

Alignment is the process of simply acting like the real you. I like to pray the Lord's Prayer from this personal place.

Father, may I now be on earth as I am in heaven.

If you have the prophetic identity of being a great earthly father, ask what things are present in your life that don't line up with that description. Impatience and quick tempers must go; love, kindness, and a nurturing spirit must be stepped into.

Alignment is what I did when I started writing sermons before I had a place to preach. This step can involve getting education or experiences that match the promise of your word. If you have a prophetic word that resonates with your heart about being a teacher, you would definitely want to stay in a place of education. You could volunteer as a class assistant at a local school. You could study the lives of great teachers. None of these actions would be considered an attempt to self-fulfill prophecy but rather as actions that align with who God says you are. Alignment manifests as our actions agree with who heaven says we are. Internal and personal preparations demonstrate I truly believe what God has said is true. Internal alignment is one of the ways we fight the Good Fight with our prophetic words.

3. Appropriation

In this case, the word "appropriation" refers to taking appropriate external steps of action and authority for who God says that you are. As I mentioned earlier, when I am traveling and doing multiple meetings, I sometimes get weary and tired. There isn't a lot of time to personally recharge. In those moments, I don't feel like I have anything to give or any ability to move in supernatural power. Those are the moments I challenge my reality with my heavenly identity. I first internally agree and align myself with what God has said by declaring something like, "Yes, this is how I feel, but it is not who I am! God says I am a culture creator and an atmosphere changer." Then I do an external act of appropriating my heavenly identity. Like putting on a coat, I put on the authority and favor appropriate to my identity and step out to live in the power, authority, and favor of who heaven says I am. Like Gideon, I win battles because God calls me a mighty warrior. It doesn't matter if I've never even owned a sword before. My history is not the prophet of my future; my heavenly identity is.

In South Africa, I processed the prophecies of a young man who had many words about evangelizing the Middle East. He came to me very concerned. "Dano," he said, "I believe these words are true, but there is a problem. My wife doesn't want to go to the Middle East and doesn't want me going either. How do I honor the Lord and my wife at the same time?"

I answered with a question, "Well, are there any Middle Eastern people here in Durban?"

He replied, "There are thousands who own businesses, especially taxis."

I advised, "Until God puts a peace in your wife's heart, every time you run into a Middle Eastern person or every time you ride in a taxi, expect a divine appointment. God is not limited to time and space. You have a God-given favor and power to influence Middle Eastern people. Start where you are and take action appropriate to who God says you are."

He took my advice and became a powerful evangelist in his own city. As far as I know, he still hasn't traveled to the Middle East, but he is no longer passively waiting on the word to come true; he is advancing in faith, experience, and authority as he prepares for the timing of the Lord. That is appropriation!

Appropriation is what you do to serve the world and people around you. It is purely an outward expression. Let me contrast the distinguishing features of alignment and appropriation once again by saying that alignment is being a king; appropriation is serving like one. Alignment is internal action and preparation; appropriation is external steps of faith. Taking action that aligns with the authority, favor, and influence of your heavenly identity will empower you to fight the Good Fight of faith.

"WARRING WITH IDENTITY" ACTIVATIONS

It's good to keep your heavenly identity statement in front of you in a variety of ways to remind you who you are and to renew your thinking in alignment with heaven. Choose one of the following activations to create a strong reminder of your heavenly identity.

Identity Collage

Gather some old magazines and cut out pictures and words that relate to your heavenly identity. Paste these images and words onto a sheet of cardstock to form an identity collage. Hang the collage in a prominent place to remind you of who you are.

Coat of Arms

Choose four to six words from your identity statement that represent the strongest ideas of who you are as a new creation. Type "coat of arms" into an online search engine. You will see several blank templates for creating a coat of arms. Choose one and print it. Now find images that represent your four to six identity definers and print them. If you prefer, draw or paint representative images on your coat of arms. There are also online programs for making a more professional-looking coat of arms. Hang your coat of arms in a prominent place to remind you of who you are. A coat of arms can also be made into a ring, a tapestry, a pendant for a necklace, a metal wall ornament, an image on a coffee mug—use your imagination.

Identity Song

Take the bullet points of your heavenly identity statement and craft them into a song or poem. Songs ingrain themselves in multiple and more diverse places in the brain resulting in a greater retention of what you sing than what you say or see. Sing the song over yourself often. If you don't sing, consider recording an audio narrative of you reading your "I Am" statement. Record it on your phone so you can play it while you travel to and from work. There is great power in hearing your own voice speak truth over yourself.

Reminder Flash Cards

Print your identity bullet points on note cards that you carry with you in a purse, backpack, or briefcase. Read aloud these statements over yourself during breaks. Meditate on what each statement is saying. Picture what a person with these qualities fully realized would look like, the things they could do, and how others would relate to them. Write on the back of the cards the impressions you receive during these meditation times.

Self-Portrait

Take a photograph of yourself or paint/draw a self-portrait that relates specifically to who God says you are. You can use your artistic talents or a photo editing software to add images or graphics relating to each of your identity bullet points. It's okay if the end result looks a little like a Picasso portrait. Frame the self-portrait and put it in a prominent place.

"WARRING WITH IDENTITY" WORKSHEET

1. What things about your heavenly identity are hardest for you to believe? Why?

_____

_____

_____

Declare over yourself regularly the truth of this identity you are finding hard to believe.

2. What current actions and attitudes do not align with who heaven is revealing you to be? What will you do about that?

_____

_____

_____

3. What actions and attitudes do you need to put on in order to align with your heavenly identity? What are some areas of education and experience you could give yourself to now that would help prepare you to manifest who God says that you are?

_____

_____

_____

_____

4. Picture the kind of person God is describing in your prophetic words. What kind of things can that person do? Imagine for a moment the kind of authority and favor a person with that heavenly identity possesses. How can you begin to appropriate the authority, favor, and influence of your heavenly identity now? Choose four actions you imagine this person you are picturing would do and list them below.

_____

_____

_____

_____

NOTES

_____

_____

_____

_____

_____

_____

_____

Prophecy releases the promises of God
that transform our realities.

PROCESSING**PROMISES**

The great missionary William Carey said:

The future is as bright as the promises of God.

Several years ago while studying quantum physics, I was struck by the fact that it is not only morally impossible for God to lie but scientifically unreasonable as well. We know that God shaped the universe with the sound of His voice. Therefore, it stands to reason that the moment God speaks, everything in the universe scrambles to take on the shape of what He just said. Even if a statement were not true a nanosecond ago, the moment God speaks it, the universe makes His words true through alignment.

For example, if God says a promotion is coming to you, you might feel that this is impossible. You might ask yourself, "How could that possibly happen?" A captain from the local fire department visited our children's church on a Sunday morning dressed in his full firefighter Class A uniform. The kids were so excited to see him. They thanked him for his service and prayed for his continued safety. After the prayer, our children's church leader asked if any of the children had a prophetic word for the fireman. One child shared that he saw the man with a gold badge. This word from the child struck the heart of the man because he was considering testing for battalion chief, and in our city, only the fire chief, deputy chief, and three battalion chiefs have gold badges.

He had been considering whether to apply for the chief position even though he had tested and been denied before. Based on the prophetic word of a child, the man moved ahead to apply for the position again and received the promotion. He now serves as one of our city's battalion chiefs.

Physical matter, situations, and people still respond to the voice that created them. This is how prophecy works. The Scripture says:

If you abide in Me, and My words abide in you, ask whatever you wish, and it will be done for you.

John 15:7, NASB

Faith opens the gate between the material and the impossible realms.

This is not just a promise; it is a law of physics. Everything in the universe—people, plants, mountains, lakes, everything—takes on its shape or form from vibrations. I believe those vibrations resonated from the voice of God as He spoke everything into existence. Therefore, the universe is shaped by the voice of the Lord. Still today, if God speaks something new, everything in the universe will scramble to take on the shape or form of what He says. When I abide in God's word and let what He is saying resonate through me, the universe will respond to my voice as if it was the voice of the Lord. Prophecy releases the promises of God that transform our reality.

Hidden within our prophetic words are the treasures of God's sovereign intentions towards us. These are things that God has promised in His goodness to fulfill, often apart from man's initiative or ability. The Bible character, Jacob, struggled with his behaviors and identity until he had a heavenly encounter. In that meeting, God reaffirmed and upgraded His promises to Jacob saying:

I will not leave you until I have done what I have promised you.

Genesis 28:15b

In this instance, God's language of promise is absolute.

Our first response to such supreme and divine determination is to believe. The disciples asked Jesus the question:

What shall we do, that we may work the works of God?[11]

Jesus replied that they must only believe on the One who was sent. This is what we must do first with the sovereign promises of God—believe in Him who promised. It may seem too small a thing at first to only believe, but if unbelief is the sin that can keep a person out of heaven, think what a great and powerful thing belief is. Belief is eternal and life-changing. Faith opens the gate between the material and the impossible realms.

Abraham's greatest failure in respect to God's prophetic word over his life was trying to act on a promise that was not primarily conditional. God didn't need Abe's help. Abraham's role was to believe the promise and keep living in harmony and alignment with the potential outcome. Abraham's efforts to advance God's promises actually obstructed and got in the way of God's intentions. It's often hard for us when we feel like we are doing nothing. But, as we have been emphasizing, belief is not nothing. To truly believe is one of the most powerful things you will ever do. It is the foundation for everything you receive in God's kingdom. Even this ability to believe is a gift of faith to all persons through the grace of a loving and good God.

> *For it is by grace you have been saved, through faith—and this is not from yourselves, it is the gift of God—*
>
> Ephesians 2:8, NASB

Let's dive into your prophetic words to mine out the treasures of sovereign promises from the God of the universe. Once again, we will start with our three sample words for practice.

---

[11] See John 6:28, NKJV.

"PROCESSING PROMISES" SAMPLE WORKSHEET

Let's revisit Samples One, Two, and Three that you used to practice looking for identity statements. Use these same samples for the following exercise.

STEP ONE:

Identify promise statements expressing God's intentions towards the recipient and underline them. Sample One is done for you below. Continue your practice on Samples Two and Three provided.

Sample One

Lord, I bless your minstrel prophet in the name of Jesus, who will be used—has been used and will be used—in an international manner to help restore the tribe of Asaph in the earth. I bless him in the Name of the Lord.

We are all general practitioners, but God gives us specialty grace. I acknowledge that the Lord has set you into the Body as one of the Asaphs that raises up the prophetic Levitical priests to set them in divine order so as to call forth a new sound.

And as the new sound comes forth, heaven responds to the sound of earth. When heaven responds to the sound of earth, heaven comes down and joins in the sound of earth. Then it becomes not only our praises ascending, but heaven has just descended into the earth realm.

So you are called as a culture creator, and an atmospheric changer to help restore the Asaph priesthood of prophetic order in Jesus' name. Amen.

Sample Two

Last night I was praying for you, Dano, and the Lord told me that you are no longer going to be known as the town drunk. Because you've gone through a season of being foolish for God, and now you are going to confound the wise.

And yeah, a change in season—literally with your identity—there is a piece of your identity that you are leaving, and you are coming into a wise thing. I saw the Lord put a helmet on your head, and it said "wisdom" across the top of it. I feel like there is incredible strategic wisdom for the nations.

I feel like you are no longer going to be known for the foolishness—and I mean the foolishness we have when we follow God—but you are going to be known for your wisdom. So you have to take off that first season that the Lord had you in and put this one on. In Jesus' name. Amen.

Sample Three

Hundreds of thousands of dollars. Hundreds of thousands of dollars. Hundreds of thousands of dollars. Hundreds of thousands of dollars. The Lord says, too, that music companies and music stores are going to give you instruments. Music stores are going to give you instruments.

The Lord says that which you are birthing of worship in the earth will be the leading edge of an evangelistic move in the countries that you are working in. You will see your sons filling stadiums. Filling them. Filling them. Filling them. You are already starting to see it. Filling stadiums. For the Lord says it is going to increase because there is a quickening spirit upon you.

The Lord says of that which He has birthed in you, He says breathe on your sons even as Jesus breathed on His disciples and sent them. Breathe on your sons. Breathe on them. Because there is a quickening spirit. And the Lord says they don't have to know everything you know for there is a quickening spirit upon them because God is saying that they have to be accelerated. You see that in the spirit yourself. You see it in the spirit yourself.

For the Lord says there are more nations in His heart for you than what you are seeing right now. More nations in His heart for you. He is going to give you sons. I can see right now a dozen nations that God has given you sons in.

He says hundreds of thousands of dollars are going to come to you. He says ask me. Ask me. Ask me for property; the answer is "yes." Ask me for recording studios; the answer is "yes" because your sons will become fathers themselves in the anointing that God has given you.

The Lord says that He gives you a quickening spirit. The reason He wants you to breathe on your sons is so that they can go back and become fathers right quick because this is a move that is going to gather pace. It's going to gather pace. Gather pace. It is going to be like a rock rolling down a hill. It is going to go fast. It is going to go fast. So the Lord says great favor is in front of you. A huge wide open space is in front of you. Explore it!

STEP TWO:

Bullet point the statements of promise and intention from all three samples in a list form. Feel free to paraphrase while using caution to not change the meaning of the statement. The promise statements from Sample One are filled in for you.

- You will help restore the tribe of Asaph in the earth.
- You have a specialty grace.
- You will call forth the new sound.
- _____
- _____
- _____
- _____
- _____

STEP THREE:

Form a crafted prayer of declaration and thanksgiving from God's promises towards the recipient of these words. This one is started for you from the promise statements of Sample One. Add to this declaration using Samples Two and Three promise statements.

Lord, thank You that You have intentionally invited me to take part in restoring the tribe of Asaph in the earth. You have graced me and equipped me for this call. Through me, You will raise up a new sound in the earth . . .

_____

_____

_____

_____

_____

_____

Now perform the same steps on your prophetic words.

"PROCESSING PROMISES" WORKSHEET

STEP ONE:

Using the same words from which you pulled out on your identity statements, identify promise statements expressing God's intentions towards you, and underline them.

STEP TWO:

List God's statements of promise and intention in a list form. Feel free to paraphrase while using caution not to change the meaning of the promise.

- _____
- _____
- _____
- _____
- _____
- _____
- _____

STEP THREE:

Form a crafted prayer of declaration and thanksgiving from God's promises towards you.

Lord, thank You that You have said . . .

_____

_____

_____

_____

NOTES

_____

_____

_____

_____

_____

_____

_____

_____

_____

_____

_____

_____

_____

_____

_____

_____

_____

_____

_____

_____

_____

_____

_____

_____

_____

_____

_____

_____

_____

_____

_____

Belief along with alignment
is necessary in order to
fight the Good Fight.

5

WARRINGWITHPROMISES

I n the last chapter, we said that the first thing we must do with God's sovereign promises is to believe. However, belief without alignment will not put you in a position to fight the Good Fight. Let me illustrate. Many years ago when I was a youth pastor, I saw a young high school student receive a prophetic word from a reliable prophet. The word said something like, "You will not need to worry about money; you will receive a sports scholarship to college." The majority of the church congregation believed the word to be true because even though the guest prophet had no prior knowledge of it, they all knew the young man he spoke over was an amazing high school baseball player. The young player believed the word of the Lord but responded in a very unwise way. He started to leave his homework undone and skip practices all the while reasoning, "What does it matter? God said I will get a scholarship."

Many of his family, friends, and leaders tried to reason with him, but he was resolute that he had to do nothing. Of course, with this kind of behavior, his grades and reputation began to slide to the point where not only did he not qualify for a scholarship, but he had to leave the team until he could bring his grades up. The mistake of the young baseball player was to assume that God would fulfill His promise to him even if he moved in the opposite direction. Though there were no specific conditions placed upon the promise through the prophetic word, the student's responsibility for alignment seemed obvious—keep playing baseball, study and work hard, and the Lord will help you get a scholarship. The baseball player also failed to see the major emphasis of the word: conquering fear and worry over not having finances for college.

God's promises to us are totally reliable yet require the same steps of warring that we applied in fighting with our identity.

- **Agree** with what God has said He will do;
- **Stay in alignment** so that the fulfillment of the promise remains possible;
- **Take appropriate steps** to show that you truly believe the word of the Lord.

Abraham and Sarah were given an impossible promise that they would have a son even in their old age. The promise was sovereign but not without human responsibility or alignment. Abraham and Sarah could have stepped out of alignment and stopped having intimate relationship, and the promise would not have come about for there was only one virgin birth. However, Abraham and Sarah also took inappropriate steps in trying to self-fulfill the prophecy through Sarah's handmaid, Hagar. In this case, Hagar and Abraham birthed a son whose descendants ended up fighting against the family of promise for thousands of years. That's a major misalignment! When God makes you a sovereign promise, you must still practice wisdom and balance. You do this by keeping yourself aligned with what God says while not trying to initiate the outcome of the promise yourself.

When God makes you a sovereign promise, you must still practice wisdom and balance.

The act of trying to self-fulfill a prophecy can seem innocent at first. Abraham and Sarah may have truly felt like they were demonstrating faith in God's promise by trying to help it come true. In actuality, it was an act of presumption. Presumption can be defined as *behavior that is arrogant or transgressing the limits of what is appropriate; acting with brash or brazen audacity.* Presumption is the arrogance of excessive self-confidence. Usually, presumption can be identified by an action that is not wholly in line with the character and nature of God. Abraham's sexual relations with Hagar might have been culturally acceptable at the time, but the heart of God is monogamy—the intimate covenant between two people. In the same way, our baseball player violated the character and nature of God when he acted lazy and unteachable. Your response to a prophetic word should never draw you away from godly behavior or the fruit of His Spirit. Anything we do in response to a prophetic word should look like something Jesus would do.

Yet, we shouldn't be so afraid of presumption that we fail to take appropriate steps of faith. Prince Jonathan, King Saul's son, once attacked an enemy outpost without a direct command from God. How was this not an act of presumption? Jonathan based his whole attack strategy upon who God had shown Himself to be. The prince said to his armor-bearer:

Nothing can hinder the LORD from saving, whether by many or by few.

1 Samuel 14:6b

Without a prophetic word, a command, or a Scripture, Jonathan acted on who he knew God to be and brought a great victory for his nation.[12] When aligning and appropriating our prophetic words, we always want to first line up with the character and nature of God. Anything outside of His nature or Scripture is a misalignment and potentially presumptuous.

Patient endurance can also be a key to seeing the promises of God fulfilled in your life. Often your situation will start moving in the opposite direction of a fresh prophetic word. It's possible that your prophetic word is being tested so that you will have the opportunity to move in faith not just reason. For the first forty years, it might have seemed reasonable for Abraham and Sarah to birth a son, but by the time they were octogenarians, it certainly seemed less probable.

Remember the prophetic dream of Joseph? The young man, Joseph, had a dream that his brothers and parents would one day bow down to him. He very unwisely shared that dream with his already jealous brothers. The brothers threw him in a pit and then sold him as a slave to a passing caravan. Joseph's situation at this point is an example of circumstances moving in the opposite direction of a prophetic word. Though Joseph lived as a slave, the favor of God made way for him to become the top slave in his master's house.

Later, the handsome young man was wrongly accused of sexual immorality by his master's wife, and Joseph was thrown into prison. Once again, his life moved in a direction that seemed opposite of his prophetic word. These challenges to our promises come from the enemy who seeks to steal, kill, and destroy anything that looks like abundant life. Yet, even the devil's tests give us an opportunity to believe from a place of genuine faith. Even in the prison, the favor and gifts of God brought Joseph to a place of promotion. The identity of God's word was proving itself true even when the circumstances of the promise were moving in an opposite direction. Eventually, Joseph became a powerful ruler in Egypt, and his family did bow down to him and reconcile with him. Patient endurance is often the best way to fight the Good Fight with your prophetic promises. Will you believe only because the outcome of the promise seems reasonable? Will you believe only when your circumstances are favorable? Or can you believe based on faith alone?

Without a prophetic word, a command, or a Scripture, Jonathan acted on who he knew God to be and brought a great victory for his nation.

---

[12] See 1 Sam 14.

Anything we do in response to a prophetic word should look like something Jesus would do.

Scripture tells us that without faith it is impossible to please God.[13] God's heroes of faith in Hebrews chapter eleven are those who believed beyond what could be seen with the natural eye and the reasoning mind. God wants to do unreasonably great things in your life. Ephesians chapter six talks about fighting while dressed in the armor of God. It instructs us to

Be strong in the Lord and his mighty power.

Ephesians 6:10

We are exhorted to "stand" some more even after we have done all we can to stand. If your circumstances move the opposite direction of your prophetic promises, do not be alarmed. Don't think that you have missed God or His promises. Stand in faith, and challenge your circumstances with God's promise. Stand against the lies and temptations of the enemy, and declare the promises of God. Stand in the strength of your heavenly identity and patiently endure until God's promises are fulfilled in you. This is the Good Fight.

---

[13] Heb 11:6.

"WARRING WITH PROMISES" WORKSHEET

1. Do you see believing as a valid work? What does believing God's promises truly mean to you?

_____

_____

_____

2. Allow yourself to imagine all of God's promises towards you fulfilled. What does that feel like? What would you be like in regard to your confidence, authority, favor, and character?

_____

_____

_____

3. What do you need to do to align yourself or to stay in alignment with what God said He would do? What things are you already doing that will remain necessary for God's word to be fulfilled in you?

_____

_____

_____

_____

_____

_____

4. In this chapter, I shared the importance of staying in alignment with the nature and character of God. Scripture says that the fruit of the Spirit is love, joy, peace, patience, kindness, goodness, faithfulness, gentleness, and self-control. Which of these are most prominently expressed in your current behavior? Which are most lacking?

_____

_____

5. Have you ever acted presumptuously or arrogantly on one of God's promises? How did that situation turn out? What were the price tags associated with that behavior? Do past failures make you fearful of stepping out in faith now? What would be an appropriate action of faith for what God has promised you?

_____

_____

_____

6. We said in this study that even without a throne, David did what a king would do. In what ways could you appropriate the favor and authority of your promise without the position or fulfillment of that promise? Figuratively speaking, how can you "serve like a king" before you receive your "throne?"

_____

_____

_____

_____

_____

NOTES

_____

_____

_____

_____

_____

_____

_____

_____

_____

_____

_____

_____

_____

Conditional promises in a prophetic
word propel us into a position of
sustained blessing.

6

PROCESSING CONDITIONS AND COMMANDS

We have examined sovereign promises, but Scripture is also filled with conditional promises. One of the most famous conditional promises quoted by Christians around the world is found in 2 Chronicles 7:14:

If my people, who are called by my name, will humble themselves and pray and seek my face and turn from their wicked ways, then I will hear from heaven, and I will forgive their sin and will heal their land.

The most important word in this conditional promise is the little word "if." In English grammar, the word "if" is most commonly used as a conjunction because it connects a main clause to a subordinate conditional clause. By using a conditional conjunction, God is showing that one clause of a promise is dependent upon the response to the specific conditions.

Conditional Clauses

Perhaps the most important conditional clause in the Bible is found in John 3:3.

Jesus answered and said to him, "Truly, truly, I say to you, unless one is born again he cannot see the kingdom of God."[14]

---

[14] NASB.

Here we find a conditional promise of utmost importance. The absolute promise of seeing the Kingdom of God is dependent on or subordinate to the required condition of first being born again.

Because God is always good, His conditional promises are not about withholding something from us but rather about creating a position of sustained blessing for us.

Why would God's promises be conditional? Because God is always good, His conditional promises are not about withholding something from us but rather about creating a position of sustained blessing for us. It does no good for God to bless us if we cannot persevere in the blessing. As a good Father, God is more interested in a life of blessing than simply a few encounters that bless. Conditions propel us into a position of sustained blessing. Conditions require alignment with a heavenly thought, value, or action.

God's heart in this is free will. God allows us to determine the boundaries of our own breakthroughs. God will not force you into the "more." He partners with us and invites us into the process of pursuing a promise. The pursuit expands us, challenges us, and takes us to new levels of skill, character, and virtue.

The primary difference between a sovereign promise and a conditional promise is found in the identification of who is initiating the process. In a sovereign promise, God makes the promise and initiates the process of fulfillment; all we must do is believe and stay in alignment with our assignment. With a conditional promise, the receiver is the initiator of the process. The process will not begin until you start fulfilling your responsibilities to the condition. Your follow-through becomes the key to your breakthrough. In this way, you are currently moving at the rate of your own obedience. Your divine acceleration is determined by how long it takes you to obey.

Command Clauses

In addition to conditional clauses, there are found in God's holy Word command clauses. We find a powerful example in the Sermon on the Mount.

But seek first his kingdom and his righteousness, and all these things will be given to you as well.

Matthew 6:33

Your follow-through becomes the key to your breakthrough. In this way, you are currently moving at the rate of your own obedience.

What are "all these things?" Houses, food, clothing, health, longevity—all of these things are conditional provisions linked to the command of seeking first the Kingdom of God and His righteousness. Conditional commands reveal the actions required to enjoy a specific benefit.

Principled Conditions

Occasionally, a prophetic promise will also contain a principled condition. Proverbs contains many principled conditions like the one found in Proverbs 19:17.

> *Whoever is kind to the poor lends to the LORD, and he will reward them for what they have done.*

God allows us to determine the boundaries of our own blessing.

Notice that the statement is not a command but a principle. Anyone who does this thing will receive this reward. Commands are not optional for an obedient believer but principled conditions are. As I said before, God allows us to determine the boundaries of our own blessing. This is true of principled conditions—you are not required to do them, but you will not receive the benefits of the promise until you do.

"PROCESSING CONDITIONS AND COMMANDS" PRACTICE

Let's start by finding the conditional promises, commands, and principles in Samples One, Two, and Three. Then practice the same technique on your own words.

STEP ONE:

Identify conditional promises and command statements. Look for words like "As you . . .", "When you . . .", and command statements like "Do this. . ." Draw a rectangle around these statements. I have done Sample One for you as an example. Your job is to find the conditional promises and command statements in the other two samples.

Sample One

Lord, I bless Your minstrel prophet in the name of Jesus, who will be used—has been used and will be used—in an international manner to help restore the tribe of Asaph in the earth. I bless him in the Name of the Lord.

We are all general practitioners, but God gives us specialty grace. I acknowledge that the Lord has set you into the Body as one of the Asaphs that raises up the prophetic Levitical priests to set them in divine order so as to call forth a new sound.

And as the new sound comes forth, heaven responds to the sound of earth. When heaven responds to the sound of earth, heaven comes down and joins in the sound of earth. Then it becomes not only our praises ascending, but heaven has just descended into the earth realm.

So you are called as a culture creator, and an atmospheric changer to help restore the Asaph priesthood of prophetic order. In Jesus' name. Amen.

Sample Two

Last night I was praying for you, Dano, and the Lord told me that you are no longer going to be known as the town drunk. Because you've gone through a season of being foolish for God, and now you are going to confound the wise.

And yeah, a change in season—literally with your identity—there is a piece of your identity that you are leaving, and you are coming into a wise thing. I saw the Lord put a helmet on your head, and it said "wisdom" across the top of it. I feel like there is incredible strategic wisdom for the nations.

I feel like you are no longer going to be known for the foolishness—and I mean the foolishness we have when we follow God—but you are going to be known for your wisdom. So you have to take off that first season that the Lord had you in and put this one on. In Jesus' name. Amen.

Sample Three

Hundreds of thousands of dollars. Hundreds of thousands of dollars. Hundreds of thousands of dollars. Hundreds of thousands of dollars. The Lord says, too, that music companies and music stores are going to give you instruments. Music stores are going to give you instruments.

The Lord says that which you are birthing of worship in the earth will be the leading edge of an evangelistic move in the countries that you are working in. You will see your sons filling stadiums. Filling them. Filling them. Filling them. You are already starting to see it. Filling stadiums. For the Lord says it is going to increase because there is a quickening spirit upon you.

The Lord says of that which He has birthed in you, He says breathe on your sons even as Jesus breathed on His disciples and sent them. Breathe on your sons. Breathe on them. Because there is a quickening spirit. And the Lord says they don't have to know everything you know for there is a quickening spirit upon them because God is saying that they have to be accelerated. You see that in the spirit yourself. You see it in the spirit yourself.

For the Lord says there are more nations in His heart for you than what you are seeing right now. More nations in His heart for you. He is going to give you sons. I can see right now a dozen nations that God has given you sons in.

He says hundreds of thousands of dollars are going to come to you. He says ask Me. Ask me. Ask Me for property; the answer is "yes." Ask Me for recording studios; the answer is "yes" because your sons will become fathers themselves in the anointing that God has given you.

The Lord says that He gives you a quickening spirit. The reason He wants you to breathe on your sons is so that they can go back and become fathers right quick because this is a move that is going to gather pace. It's going to gather pace. Gather pace. It is going to be like a rock rolling down a hill. It is going to go fast. It is going to go fast. So the Lord says great favor is in front of you. A huge wide open space is in front of you. Explore it!

These conditional and principled commands can be a little more complex to sort out. Now that you've given it a try, I want to offer more examples of what I found in processing Samples Two and Three. You may have found more, but check your answers against these few examples.

CONDITIONAL COMMANDS

So you have to take off that first season that the Lord had you in and put this one on.

The promise is a new season of being known for wisdom.

The command is to take off the first season of foolishness and put this new one on.

The promise will not happen until the command is obeyed.

He says hundreds of thousands of dollars are going to come to you. He says, "Ask Me. Ask Me. Ask Me for property; the answer is "yes." Ask Me for recording studios; the answer is "yes" because your sons will become fathers themselves in the anointing that God has given you.

The promise is hundreds of thousands of dollars, property, and recording studios

The command is, "Ask me."

The promise will not happen until the command is obeyed.

PRINCIPLED COMMANDS

Set them in divine order so as to call forth a new sound. And as the new sound comes forth, heaven responds to the sound of earth. And when heaven responds to the sound of earth, heaven comes down and joins in the sound of earth.

The principle is that heaven responds to the new sound/sound of the earth.

The requirement is to call forth a new sound.

As the requirement is met, the principle will be activated.

STEP TWO:

Put the findings from each of the words you are processing into one table with the required action on one side and the promised outcome on the other. I have started filling in the table from our sample exercises. Complete the table with the information you discovered from the sample words.

Action	Outcome
Call forth a new sound	New songs will arise
Restore the Asaph prophetic order	Raise up worship leaders in nations

STEP THREE:

Create a MAP (Ministry Action Plan) from the conditions you highlighted. Once again, I have started the exercise for you. Use your table to complete the action plan.

I will call forth the new sound prophetically each time I'm in a nation.

I will look for Asaph's that carry the prophetic songs for nations.

I will _____

I will _____

I will _____

Now, use the following worksheet to try these techniques on your own prophetic words.

"PROCESSING CONDITIONS AND COMMANDS" WORKSHEET

STEP ONE:

Identify conditional promises, command statements, and principled conditions. Look for words like: after, as you, as long as, as soon as, assuming that, before, if, if only, in order to, once, only if, provided that, so long as, therefore, unless, until, while you, when, whenever, wherever.

Action verbs connected to a specific promise are cues that a conditional command may be present. Draw a rectangle around any of these conditional statements of promise.

STEP TWO:

Put your conditional promises into a table with the required action on one side and the promised outcome on the other.

Action	Outcome

STEP THREE:

Create a MAP (Ministry Action Plan) from your listed conditions.

I will _____

I will _____

I will _____

I will _____

I will _____

I will _____

NOTES

_____

_____

_____

_____

_____

_____

_____

Understanding when to decree and
when to act is the key to fighting the
Good Fight.

7

WARRING WITH CONDITIONS AND COMMANDS

'Ve watched people war with their prophetic words for many years. One of the common errors I have seen is that believers sometimes try to declare and decree a promise or command into fruition when it actually requires an action of faith. With sovereign promises, we must fight the urge to take off in self-appointed actions. We stand in faith and stay in alignment, but we do not initiate the process of fulfilling those promises. Declarations and decrees are appropriate actions for someone who is standing on a sovereign prophetic promise. This is not necessarily true with a conditional promise. In a conditional promise, command, or principle, your faith is expressed through your works of faith not just through declarations of faith. Declarations and decrees without follow-through land like empty words. Never allow your beliefs to become merely spiritual fantasies or vain imaginations. You combat this by acting on what you believe.

The book of James teaches the importance of backing up faith with works.

You believe that there is a God. Good! Even the demons believe that—and shudder. You foolish person, do you want evidence that faith without deeds is useless? Was not our father Abraham considered righteous for what he did when he offered his son Isaac on the altar? You see that his faith and his actions were working together, and his faith was made complete by what he did.

James 2:19-21

Let me use a Bible example to illustrate the difference between response to a sovereign promise and appropriate action for a conditional promise. Twice in Scripture Moses was commanded to bring forth water from a rock for a thirsty nation. The first time, God told Moses to strike the rock and water would pour forth from it.[15] Striking the rock can be seen as his acting on a conditional promise—unless Moses did the action of faith, the water would not pour out for the people. The next time the people were thirsty, Moses was commanded to speak to the rock.[16] Speaking to the rock is like decreeing or agreeing with a sovereign promise. Moses did not have to take a physical action; he only needed to align his words with what God had said. However, Moses disobeyed in this second occurrence when he struck the rock, thereby, dishonoring the Lord and showing a lack of trust. This unfortunate choice eventually prevented Moses from being the one to bring the community he served into the land of promise. Metaphorically, you must know when to speak to the rock—a sovereign promise—and when to strike it with action—a conditional command, principle, or promise. Understanding when to decree and when to act is a key to fighting the Good Fight.

> **In a conditional promise, command, or principle, your faith is expressed through your works of faith, not just through declarations of faith.**

Mindsets, Cautions, and Actions

There are three areas under which I categorize the processing of conditional promises: mindsets, cautions, and actions.

Mindsets

The first category has to do with mindsets—a fixed belief system held by someone. Sometimes our mindsets need to be transformed. Prophetic words will often dictate the way we must think. Abraham had to see himself as an exalted father not a barren old man. Gideon needed to forfeit the idea of being the least and the smallest of his people and renew his mind to see himself as a warrior who could lead Israel to victory. David had to overcome the fact that he was hated and hunted rather than celebrated as the next king of Israel. Still, he had to see himself as anointed to be king.

In prophetic processing, I like to list separately any mindsets that God draws attention to. From Sample Two I would list the following:

---

[15] See Exod 17:6.
[16] See Num 20:7.

Mindset: I will choose to think of myself as a man of wisdom.

Cautions

The second category for processing conditions is identifying any cautions. Embedded in our prophetic words may be gentle or direct warnings of behavior that don't line up with where God is leading. Pay attention to the cautions the Lord reveals in your prophetic words. God commanded Gideon to not be afraid because he would surely deliver Israel. This was a caution—don't let fear get in the way!

Here is an example of a caution from Sample Three:

> Caution: I won't restrict or judge people according to how much they know. I will make sure that I don't think my spiritual sons have to know everything I know to be effective. I will breathe on them and trust the impartation and acceleration of the Spirit.

Actions

Actions are the third category for processing conditional promises. Take the time to list out any actions you need to take to accelerate the promise God has given. The smallest act of obedience in the direction of God's commands can be a huge catalyst for change and divine appointments. Gideon's first action step was to tear down his father's false altar and build a legitimate altar to the Lord. This action step served as a catalyst for later fulfillment of promises because God wanted to show that the victory was from the Lord.

The smallest act of obedience in the direction of God's commands can be a huge catalyst for change and divine appointments.

These examples of necessary actions come from Samples Two and Three:

- Action: I will make a regular habit of asking God for hundreds of thousands of dollars, properties, and recording studios.
- Action: I will call forth the new sound prophetically each time I am in another nation.

These three categories—mindsets, cautions, and actions—help form a ministry action plan or MAP It's a way of knowing how to move forward with prophetic words. Now it's your turn to look through your prophetic words in search of these three categories of response.

"WARRING WITH CONDITIONS AND COMMANDS" WORKSHEET

Go through the conditional promises you've uncovered in the prophetic words you are processing. Divide them into the three categories, listing them in the form of an action statement as in the examples shown in chapter seven.

1. Mindsets

_____

_____

_____

_____

2. Cautions

_____

_____

_____

_____

3. Actions

_____

_____

_____

_____

NOTES

_____

_____

_____

_____

_____

_____

_____

_____

_____

_____

_____

_____

_____

_____

_____

THE GOOD FIGHT

Faith opens the gate between the
material and impossible realms.

PROCESSING
TIMES AND SEASONS

Have you ever been late for something important because you forgot to set a clock back one hour at the start of daylight savings time? Or have you ever missed an important event like a wedding, party, or job interview because you wrote the time down wrong? Prophetic processing is not just about knowing what to do; it is knowing what to do in the right time and season. One of the most well-known verses in the Bible on this subject is found in the first book of Chronicles.

> *Of the sons of Issachar,* **men who understood the times**, *with knowledge of what Israel should do, their chiefs were two hundred; and all their kinsmen were at their command.*
>
> 1 Chronicles 12:32, NASB, emphasis added

This verse reveals another goal in prophetic processing. We are looking to gain the wisdom of the spirit of Issachar, to become people who understand the times and know what to do. We want to look for the right things in the right season.

Jesus rebuked the religious leaders for looking for a sign but not understanding the season they were in.

> *The Pharisees and Sadducees came to Jesus and tested him by asking him to show them a sign from heaven. He replied, "When evening comes, you say, 'It will be fair weather, for the sky is red,' and in the morning, 'Today it will be stormy, for the sky is red and overcast.' You know how to interpret the appearance of the sky, but you cannot interpret the signs of the times."*
>
> Matthew 16:1-3

Prophetic processing is not just about knowing what to do; it is knowing what to do in the right time and season.

This statement of Jesus' implies an expectation that His people would learn how to discern times and seasons. The Lord wants each one of us to understand the time and the season we are living in to maximize the benefits and promises of that specific season. Some blessings are time sensitive—they only work in certain seasons. Jesus' physical ministry on the earth was a very short period of time. Most of the Pharisees and Sadducees missed the window of properly interacting with God in the season of His physical ministry on the earth. What a tragedy to miss one of the greatest manifestations of God's nature, power, and love because they were living out of season.

Daniel was a prophet who understood the times and knew what to do.

> *In the first year of his reign, I, Daniel, understood from the Scriptures, according to the word of the LORD given to Jeremiah the prophet, that the desolation of Jerusalem would last seventy years. So I turned to the Lord God and pleaded with him in prayer and petition, in fasting, and in sackcloth and ashes.*
>
> Daniel 9:2-3

Daniel used the prophecies of Jeremiah that predicted a seventy-year captivity to position himself to do the right thing at the right time. He began to align in prayer, petition, fasting, and repentance for the word of the Lord to be fulfilled according to the timing of the promise. Daniel's actions directed at that promise would be entirely out of place even two or three years earlier. By understanding the prophetic times and seasons, Daniel was found doing the right thing in the right time. God desires that kind of alignment with times and season for every one of us.

To understand your times and seasons, simply look for timing indicators in your prophetic words. The following are types of timing words:

> after, at hand, at that time, before, day, decade, delay, during, earlier, era, every day, future, hour, in time, later, minute, momentary, now, new, past, present, season, soon, someday, sometime, sunrise, sunset, then, times, today, tomorrow, weeks, when, yesterday

These words will help indicate the times and seasons for each of your prophetic promises. We are looking specifically to understand four types of times and seasons:

1. What is in the *past* or what has already been established?
2. What is current or *present?* What are your *now* words?
3. What is *soon* coming?
4. What things speak to a *future* time or season?

In becoming aware of the times and seasons within our words, we are less likely to waste time contending religiously for things that God already says we have. We can also rest in the things that relate specifically to our current season. Regarding things that are coming soon, we can anticipate, expect, and align ourselves with what the Lord promises is in our near future. There is also a rest in knowing what things we can put away for a season that is yet to come. Perhaps there is the awareness of long-term preparations to make, and yet it is also a liberating feeling to be released from the urgent pressure of pursuing promises that are actually meant for a different season.

"PROCESSING TIMES AND SEASONS" PRACTICE

STEP ONE:

Identify time and season indicators by drawing a triangle around any timing words. By way of example, Sample One is done for you. Look for and mark any timing indicators you find in Samples Two and Three.

Note: Of course, every verb has a past, present, or future tense attached to it. Mark only the verbs that to you personally show a strong sense of timing. For instance, in the first paragraph of Sample One, I marked the verbs "will be" and "has been." In context, these verbs give a stronger emphasis on timing of past and future happenings that I feel I want to pay attention to.

Sample One

Lord, I bless Your minstrel prophet in the name of Jesus, who will be used—has been used and will be used—in an international manner to help restore the tribe of Asaph in the earth. I bless him in the Name of the Lord.

We are all general practitioners, but God gives us specialty grace. I acknowledge that the Lord has set you into the Body as one of the Asaphs that raises up the prophetic Levitical priests to set them in divine order so as to call forth a new sound.

And as the new sound comes forth, heaven responds to the sound of earth. When heaven responds to the sound of earth, heaven comes down and joins in the sound of earth. Then it becomes not only our praises ascending, but heaven has just descended into the earth realm.

So you are called as a culture creator, and an atmospheric changer to help restore the Asaph priesthood of prophetic order. In Jesus' name. Amen.

Sample Two

Last night I was praying for you, Dano, and the Lord told me that you are no longer going to be known as the town drunk. Because you've gone through a season of being foolish for God, and now you are going to confound the wise.

And yeah, a change in season—literally with your identity—there is a piece of your identity that you are leaving, and you are coming into a wise thing. I saw the Lord put a helmet on your head, and it said "wisdom" across the top of it. I feel like there is incredible strategic wisdom for the nations.

I feel like you are no longer going to be known for the foolishness—and I mean the foolishness we have when we follow God—but you are going to be known for your wisdom. So you have to take off that first season that the Lord had you in and put this one on. In Jesus' name. Amen.

Sample Three

Hundreds of thousands of dollars. Hundreds of thousands of dollars. Hundreds of thousands of dollars. Hundreds of thousands of dollars. The Lord says, too, that music companies and music stores are going to give you instruments. Music stores are going to give you instruments.

The Lord says that which you are birthing of worship in the earth will be the leading edge of an evangelistic move in the countries that you are working in. You will see your sons filling stadiums. Filling them. Filling them. Filling them. You are already starting to see it. Filling stadiums. For the Lord says it is going to increase because there is a quickening spirit upon you.

The Lord says of that which He has birthed in you, He says breathe on your sons even as Jesus breathed on His disciples and sent them. Breathe on your sons. Breathe on them. Because there is a quickening spirit. And the Lord says they don't have to know everything you know for there is a quickening spirit upon them because God is saying that they have to be accelerated. You see that in the spirit yourself. You see it in the spirit yourself.

For the Lord says there are more nations in His heart for you than what you are seeing right now. More nations in His heart for you. He is going to give you sons. I can see right now a dozen nations that God has given you sons in.

THE GOOD FIGHT

He says hundreds of thousands of dollars are going to come to you. He says ask Me. Ask Me. Ask Me for property; the answer is "yes." Ask Me for recording studios; the answer is "yes" because your sons will become fathers themselves in the anointing that God has given you.

The Lord says that He gives you a quickening spirit. The reason He wants you to breathe on your sons is so that they can go back and become fathers right quick because this is a move that is going to gather pace. It's going to gather pace. Gather pace. It is going to be like a rock rolling down a hill. It is going to go fast. It is going to go fast. So the Lord says great favor is in front of you. A huge wide open space is in front of you. Explore it!

STEP TWO:

Graph times and seasons by placing any promises related to specific timing words within their appropriate categories. Sample One is done for you. Complete the graph using timing words from Samples Two and Three.

Times and Seasons Graph

Past	Present	Soon	Later
Has been used . . .		Will be used . . .	
The Lord has set you . . .			
		As the new song . . . When heaven . . . Then it will be . . .	

90

STEP THREE:

- Create a declaration of times and seasons.
- I have been . . .
- I am . . .
- I will soon . . .
- One day . . .

The following is an example of a declaration taken from the times and seasons statements from Sample One. Add to the declaration using what you learned from the timing words in Sample Two and Three.

> God has already set me as an Asaph in the Body of Christ. I have been used and will continue to be used to restore the Levitical priesthood in the earth. As I call forth the new sound, heaven will respond, and then the realities of heaven will descend to the earth realm . . .

_____

_____

_____

_____

_____

Using the following worksheet, it's time to apply these same processes to your own prophetic words.

"PROCESSING TIMES AND SEASONS" WORKSHEET

STEP ONE:

Put a triangle around any timing words you spot in your prophetic words and note the phrases they are attached to. Here is a list of some common timing words:

after, at hand, at that time, before, coming, day, decade, delay, during, earlier, era, every day, future, hour, in time, later, minute, momentary, now, new, past, present, season, soon, someday, sometime, sunrise, sunset, then, times, today, tomorrow, weeks, when, yesterday

STEP TWO:

Put these timing phrases into a times and seasons graph.

Times and Seasons Graph

Past	Present	Soon	Later

STEP THREE:

Create a declaration of timing for yourself.

I'm no longer . . .

_____

_____

_____

I am now . . .

_____

_____

_____

I will soon . . .

_____

_____

_____

In the future, I will . . .

_____

_____

_____

We war with the times and seasons
of our prophetic words by choosing
peace over pressure.

WARRING WITH TIMES AND SEASONS

Any good fight requires good timing. By now, you should understand that the New Testament focus of prophecy is to encourage, strengthen, and comfort.[17] A peculiar thing about prophetic words and how we view timing is that a word in the wrong season doesn't always meet that encouragement criteria. I have met so many people who felt intimidated or confined by a prophetic word. They either felt pressure to make it come true or frustration that their reality seemed so far from the promise. Pressure or frustration resulting from your prophetic words are usually symptoms of either not judging the word correctly or of not understanding the times and seasons associated with your prophetic words.

Knowing what season you have come out of, what season you are in, and what season is next brings a lot of strength and comfort. It's also very comforting to know when some of your bigger words are speaking to a future season. A right view of your times and seasons takes undue pressure off as you remember that God speaks to you through a much bigger view of time. When we assign a right word to a wrong season, it will manifest in a sense of shame for failing to measure up to or achieve the prophetic word that was spoken. Shame, guilt, pressure, or feelings of failure are signs that something is wrong. Obviously, I'm not speaking here to someone who is deliberately running in a direction opposite of their prophetic words; I'm speaking to the person who is conscientiously pursuing and agreeing with their words but not gaining a lot of traction. Resist the temptation to feel like a failure or like time is running out.

---

[17] 1 Cor 14:3.

God has made room for you to fulfill every promise you are meant to accomplish within your lifetime.

I have a friend in his sixties who often says, "I am the perfect age for what God has for me." That is a great position to take. God knows your times and your seasons, and He has made room for you to fulfill every promise you are meant to accomplish within your lifetime. I love the wise words from the book of Ecclesiastes:

There is a time for everything and a season for every activity under the heavens.

3:1

My mentor used to say, "God can prepare a person their whole life to do more in one day than others do in their whole life."[18]

We war with the times and seasons of our prophetic words by choosing peace over pressure. If your prophetic words are not encouraging, strengthening, and comforting you, then consider that you may be misinterpreting your current season. Break agreement with the pressure to perform. Disavow the lie of being too late. Make friends with time; refuse to let it be your foe. God has created a time and a season for every activity He has promised you.

Failure is never fatal in God's grace.

Since we understand that fighting the Good Fight is also about timing, let's do some exercises to help you make peace with your times and seasons.

---

[18] Cleddie Keith, Florence, Kentucky.

"WARRING WITH TIMES AND SEASONS" WORKSHEET

1. Review words that speak to your past season. Take time to meditate on the accomplishments of the last season. Thank God for the grace that carried you through and enabled you in the former season. Remember and recount any manifestations of the goodness of the Lord in the season that you have come out of. Receive grace and forgiveness for any opportunities you may feel were misused or missed. Failure is never fatal in God's grace. Let any past pains propel you to new places of wisdom and understanding. Don't forget to acknowledge that becoming aware of places where you "missed it" is one of the signs of growth and strength. You are a different person than when the last season began. You are stronger and wiser. Thank the Lord for all He has done to bring you through the last season.

Write out the greatest triumph or revelation you received from the season you were last in.

_____

_____

_____

2. Next, reflect on your current season. What are the strengths and promises God is affirming and confirming concerning where you are now? How do your prophetic words define this season? Does your evaluation agree with what God is saying about this season?

Write a short definition of your current season according to what God is saying about it.

_____

_____

_____

_____

3. Practice aligning your view with what God is revealing. Make time your friend. Cast off pressure and take on the peace of God that passes understanding. Speak over yourself, "I am the perfect age for everything God has for me in this season." Declare that this is a good season. Practice enjoying the season you are in. Confess that you are a redeemer of time. Time does not rule you; time serves you. God makes everything beautiful in its time.[19] Practice fully embracing the beauty that God has placed in this current season.

Write out what you most enjoy in your current season.

_____

_____

_____

4. Review the mindsets, cautions, and actions of your Ministry Action Plan from the "Warring With Conditional Promises" chapter. These are your keys to stepping into your next season. Reflect on how you can use your time to engage with these mindsets, cautions, and actions. You may want to set some short-range goals for activating these three areas. For instance, I may set the goal of asking God daily for hundreds of thousands of dollars for the next ninety days. Another goal might be to call forth the new sound in a foreign nation within the next six months. Setting timelines on your action steps helps to keep your prophetic acceleration moving forward. Take time now to thank the Lord that He has revealed these keys to usher you into another season of growth and expansion. Embrace the grace to step fully from one season to the next.

Write out one short-term goal you will begin acting on now to move you toward your coming season.

_____

_____

_____

_____

_____

[19] Eccl 8:9.

5. Now look to your future. There are some big and amazing words over your life. Some of them speak to a future season. Practice believing that there is time to fulfill those words. Ask the Lord if there are any "baby steps" He wants you to take now that will help prepare you for your future season. Reflect on any victories from your past that may have prepared you for your future. Do you remember how David recounted his victories over the lion and the bear before facing the giants of his future? What victories from your past are meant to propel you towards your future? Thank God for what is coming. Thank Him for His ability to bring you into your land and season of promise. God is well able to fulfill His promises to you. Take some time to praise Him for His goodness.

Write down any past victories that you believe relate to your future promises.

_____

_____

_____

NOTES

_____

_____

_____

_____

_____

_____

Your gift works everywhere on everyone,
but it works best somewhere on
someone.

10

PROCESSING
SPHERES○OF INFLUENCE

Every gift and every assignment has a specific sphere of influence where it works most effectively. Your gift works everywhere on everyone, but it works best somewhere on someone. The same applies to your prophetic promises. Your prophetic promises usually have a specific assignment to a place or people group.

People are often under the mistaken idea that God has given us all power and authority everywhere. God gives you all power and authority in the areas He has assigned you. You don't have all power and authority when you visit my house. You don't have all power and authority to drive any way you want to on the highway. However, God has given you all power and authority within an assigned sphere of influence.

Finding your sphere of influence is like discovering a sweet spot of service where you are uniquely equipped and gifted to operate. Your sphere of influence is where you possess the most favor, authority, and influence. The more you function within your sphere of influence, the more enjoyable life can be. This is because you are especially equipped with grace, gifts, and power to be effective in that place. In the King James Version, sphere of influence is called your "measure of the rule."

But we will not boast of things without measure, but according to the **measure of the rule** *which God hath distributed to us . . .*

2 Corinthians 10:13, KJV, emphasis added

There are three different spheres or measures of rule I like to focus on—demographic, geographic, and sociographic. A demographic sphere is a certain type of person; a geographic sphere is a specific place; a sociographic sphere is an interest group. Let's look at the biblical basis for spheres of influence and the types of spheres in a little more detail so that you can locate these treasures within your prophetic words.

Demographic Sphere

Paul the Apostle said that he wasn't an apostle to everyone but to a specific group of people.

Even though I may not be an apostle to others, surely I am to you!

1 Corinthians 9:2

In the book of Romans Paul declares:

I am talking to you Gentiles. Inasmuch as I am the apostle to the Gentiles . . .

Romans 11:13

Paul was welcome to speak to anyone and everyone about Jesus and often did. We see examples of him speaking to Jewish people in the Scripture, but here he confesses that his assigned sphere of influence is to the Gentile people. In his second letter to the Corinthian church, Paul said that he would confine his boasting to the field of service God had assigned to him.[20] We can see that Paul understood his authority and assignment within a specific demographic sphere.

Jesus had a specific sphere of influence that He was sensitive to. Remember when the Canaanite woman came and asked Jesus for healing for her demon-possessed daughter? Jesus responded:

I was sent only to the lost sheep of Israel.

Matthew 15:24

---

[20] 2 Cor 10:13.

That sounds harsh, doesn't it? Why would Jesus deny this woman based upon her race? Remember that Jesus came to earth as a person under authority. He was careful to confine most of His ministry to the demographic of the lost sheep of Israel. Still, Jesus had freedom to act outside of His assignment. Because of the woman's faith and desperation, Jesus helped her, and her child was totally set free. But the fact is that Jesus was careful to stay within the demographic sphere that God had assigned to Him.

A demographic sphere could be with an age group. You might find that you are especially gifted for children, senior citizens, youth, married people, or people from a specific nation or ethnic group. This sphere of influence manifests as a grace and enjoyment of interacting with this sector of people. Not everyone enjoys hanging out with a bunch of little children, but some people love it. I know a young lady who is fascinated by the stories of senior citizens. She can listen for hours on end and genuinely enjoys their first-hand historical accounts. That's not just a personality thing; it is a sphere of influence that she is uniquely gifted and graced for.

> **Finding your sphere of influence is like discovering a sweet spot of service where you are uniquely equipped and gifted to operate.**

There are also distinctions within certain cultures that you can have a special grace or a lack of grace for. Tribal cultures usually move at a much slower pace with an emphasis on story and relationships. To someone without a tribal grace or assignment, this cultural bend could seem boring, but to someone with this sphere of influence, every word is precious. City cultures move fast and tend to converse around the bottom line. To someone with a city grace and calling, this is an exciting acceleration; to someone without this sphere of influence, it can seem to be merely a rat race. Each of these spheres requires a certain gift and grace. These gifts and graces will often show up in your prophetic words and promises.

Geographic Sphere

We also find people with promises and assignments in certain geographical spheres. Abraham was sent to a specific and promised designation of land that became known as the Promised Land. The same was true for the children of Israel. Their prophetic promise applied to a specific geographical region. God is good everywhere, but there were special prophetic promises made to this nation that would only come true within the geographical boundaries of their Promised Land.

A geographic sphere does not have to be limited to one place. Jeremiah was called to be a prophet to many nations.

*Before I formed you in the womb I knew you, before you were born I set you apart; I appointed you as a prophet to the **nations**.*

Jeremiah 1:5, emphasis added

While Jeremiah had a call to a very broad geographical sphere, the prophet Samuel was assigned to very specific borders.

And all Israel from Dan to Beersheba recognized that Samuel was attested as a prophet of the LORD.

1 Samuel 3:20

When I travel, I look for countries where I seem to have an unusual grace, favor, and authority. By the grace of God, I can minister effectively anywhere, but I'm looking for that sweet spot of the measure of my rule—my sphere of influence.

A geographical sphere could be within the boundary of your own home. You can have an assignment from God to serve your own household, creating an atmosphere of love and peace, mentoring and discipling your children, or hosting people with a supernatural gift of hospitality. A geographical sphere could be a burden for the neighborhood you live in, or your city, state, region, nation, or continent.

A geographical sphere will manifest as a love and honor for a specific territory. It's like finding your home—your land—a space that makes you feel connected, secure, or significant. Love and honor attract the prophetic, so it is not uncommon for these geographic spheres to be confirmed or defined within your prophetic promises.

Sociographic Sphere

There are also examples of assignments to a certain interest group within society. A sociographic sphere applies to an interest within society not limited to a certain people or place. Asaph, Jeduthan, and Heman were prophetic trainers specifically called to serve musicians, singers, and temple servants. It didn't matter if they were young or old or where they were from—the calling was to musicians and servants in the tabernacle of David.

Daniel's prophetic destiny was expressed in serving world leaders under four different kingdoms. Daniel had a sociographic government sphere of influence that could serve leaders of different ages and from four different countries. Joseph's prophetic gift shone in making business people and government leaders prosperous. Wherever he went and whatever he was assigned to, he created systems for his oversight to prosper. In these two biblical examples, we see Daniel had a government sphere of influence, and Joseph had a business (financial) sphere of influence that affected both businessmen and government.

Remember that none of this means that your promises and gifts will not work in places outside your sphere of influence nor that they are effective only with specific people. However, it is true that your gifts, graces, and promises often have a sphere where they function best.

Some of these sociographic spheres could fall into the categories of what has been called the "seven mountains of society." The seven major areas that affect society are business, government, family, education, media, arts and entertainment, and religion. Keep in mind, though, that sociographic spheres are certainly not limited to these seven broad categories. You might be called to serve street people, surfers, millionaires, singles, orphans, runaways, sports figures, celebrities—the list would be endless. The defining factor of the sociographic sphere is that it is not limited to a place, age, gender, or racial boundary unless it is combined with a calling to a specific geographic or demographic sphere. A sociographic sphere manifests as a love and interest in a specific group within society.

One of the ways that you discover any field of service, measure of rule, or sphere of influence is by finding designations or assignments within your prophetic words. Let's start this exploration with the sample words I have provided for you.

"PROCESSING SPHERES OF INFLUENCE" PRACTICE

STEP ONE:

Look for any people, places, or special areas of interests. Place a dotted line under any indicators of spheres of influence. Sample One has been started for you.

Sample One

Lord, I bless Your minstrel prophet in the name of Jesus, that will be used—has been used—and will be used in an international manner to help restore the tribe of Asaph in the earth. I bless him in the name of the Lord.

We are all general practitioners, but God gives us specialty grace you see. And I just acknowledge that the Lord has set you into the Body as one of the Asaphs that raises up the prophetic Levitical priests to set them in divine order so as to call forth a new sound.

And as the new sound comes forth, heaven responds to the sound of earth. And when heaven responds to the sound of earth, heaven comes down and joins in the sound of earth. Then, it becomes not only our praises ascending but heaven has just descended into the earth realm.

So you are called as a culture creator, and an atmospheric changer to help restore the Asaph priesthood of prophetic order. In Jesus' Name. Amen.

1. Would you say there were any location or geographic definers in this prophetic word? If so, what were the words that talked about a specific location?

_____

_____

_____

_____

2. Also, did you notice that this word is a promise for a specific interest group? The promises would not apply to everyone. What is the sociographic sphere or specific interest group that this prophetic word speaks to?

_____

_____

3. Check the other two sample words for people, places, and interest groups that might define a sphere of influence. See if Samples Two and Three point to the same or different spheres of influence as Sample One. Place a dotted line beneath any words that seem to assign attention to a people, place, or interest.

Sample Two

Last night I was praying for you, Dano, and the Lord told me that you are no longer going to be known as the town drunk. Because you've gone through a season of being foolish for God, and now you are going to confound the wise.

And yeah, a change in season—literally with your identity—there is a piece of your identity that you are leaving, and you are coming into a wise thing. I saw the Lord put a helmet on your head, and it said "wisdom" across the top of it. I feel like there is incredible strategic wisdom for the nations.

I feel like you are no longer going to be known for the foolishness—and I mean the foolishness we have when we follow God—but you are going to be known for your wisdom. So you have to take off that first season that the Lord had you in and put this one on. In Jesus' name. Amen.

Sample Three

Hundreds of thousands of dollars. Hundreds of thousands of dollars. Hundreds of thousands of dollars. Hundreds of thousands of dollars. The Lord says, too, that music companies and music stores are going to give you instruments. Music stores are going to give you instruments.

The Lord says that which you are birthing of worship in the earth will be the leading edge of an evangelistic move in the countries that you are working in.

You will see your sons filling stadiums. Filling them. Filling them. Filling them. You are already starting to see it. Filling stadiums. For the Lord says it is going to increase because there is a quickening spirit upon you.

The Lord says of that which He has birthed in you, He says breathe on your sons even as Jesus breathed on his disciples and sent them. Breathe on your sons. Breathe on them. Because there is a quickening spirit. And the Lord says they don't have to know everything you know for there is a quickening spirit upon them because God is saying that they have to be accelerated. You see that in the spirit yourself. You see it in the spirit yourself.

For the Lord says there are more nations in His heart for you than what you are seeing right now. More nations in His heart for you. He is going to give you sons. I can see right now a dozen nations that God has given you sons in.

He says hundreds of thousands of dollars are going to come to you. He says ask Me. Ask Me. Ask Me for property; the answer is "yes." Ask Me for recording studios; the answer is "yes" because your sons will become fathers themselves in the anointing that God has given you.

The Lord says that He gives you a quickening spirit. The reason He wants you to breathe on your sons is so that they can go back and become fathers right quick because this is a move that is going to gather pace. It's going to gather pace. Gather pace. It is going to be like a rock rolling down a hill. It is going to go fast. It is going to go fast. So the Lord says great favor is in front of you. A huge wide open space is in front of you. Explore it!

STEP TWO:

List the information you underscored in the space provided below.

- tribe of Asaph
- in the earth
- Levitical priests, Asaph priesthood

_____

_____

_____

_____

STEP THREE:

Categorize the information of people, places and interest groups into the three paragraphs below.

Geographic Sphere: Where should I focus my efforts?

_____

_____

Demographic Sphere: Who should I be serving?

_____

_____

Sociographic Sphere: What am I best equipped to do?

_____

_____

Using the following worksheet, now let's apply these principles to your own prophetic words.

"PROCESSING SPHERES OF INFLUENCE" WORKSHEET

STEP ONE:

Look for any assignment of spheres involving people, places, or special areas of interests within your prophetic words. Underscore them with a dotted line.

STEP TWO:

List the information you underscored in the space provided below.

- _____
- _____
- _____
- _____
- _____
- _____

STEP THREE:

Categorize the information of people, places, and interest groups into the spaces below.

Geographic Sphere: Where should I focus my efforts?

_____

_____

Demographic Sphere: Who should I be serving?

_____

_____

Sociographic Sphere: What am I best equipped to do?

_____

_____

NOTES

_____

_____

_____

_____

_____

_____

_____

_____

_____

Understanding your sphere of influence
gives you the direction and focus you
need to fight the Good Fight God has
laid out for you.

WARRING WITH
SPHERES OF INFLUENCE

Passion and focus make champions out of ordinary people. In his book on mastery, Robert Greene says:

The time that leads to mastery is dependent upon the intensity of the focus. [21]

Motivational speaker, Zig Ziglar, says:

Lack of direction not lack of time is the greatest problem.

Fighting the Good Fight requires a clear focus and direction. *What am I fighting for? What is the aim of my race?* Champions and warriors know what to focus on and in what direction to go. I like the way the Apostle Paul stated this.

Therefore I do not run like someone running aimlessly; I do not fight like a boxer beating the air.

1 Corinthians 9:26

---

[21] Greene, Robert. *Mastery.* Penguin Books, New York, NY, 2012.

To fight the Good Fight, I must know what my fight or my focus is. That is why mining the treasures of your spheres of influence can be so helpful—it gives your fight a focus. Knowing my people, my place, or my service within society gives me a purpose for being. Once I know my primary sphere of influence, I can apply the majority of my time, energy, and talents to serving this field. We can get a passion or a vision for many good things to do in the earth. How do we know which one to give ourselves to? How do we keep from being spread too thin or over-extending ourselves in too many areas? Understanding your sphere of influence gives you the direction and focus you need to fight the Good Fight God has laid out for you.

Safe Guards

Before we get much farther in this discussion, let's make sure we have some safe guards in place. The spheres of influence revealed in your prophetic words should be something you are interested in or excited about it. It should line up with your gifts and graces in a way that releases positive thoughts and feelings. At the same time, occasionally a prophetic word can speak to a potential blind spot where you don't feel the excitement or agreement right away. This was the case for me when I received a prophetic word to go India.

When I was a young man, I read a wonderful book about a missionary in India. The book truly impacted my life, but it shared living and ministry conditions so horrible that I made an inner vow that I would go anywhere in the world God sent me except India. Fast-forward twenty-five years, and I am traveling the world as a trainer and revivalist. I had a prayer partner who was a businessman. He used his extra profits to hold training and refreshing events for pastors. One day my friend came to me with a need.

"Dano, I have a pastor's conference coming up, and my speaker had to cancel." I knew he was asking if I could fill the vacancy for him.

"When is it?" I asked. My friend gave me the dates and I saw that those specific dates were clear on my calendar. "It looks like I could do that for you," I replied with a smile. "Oh, where is it, by the way?" I queried.

"India," he answered.

Now it was too late, I had already given my word. A strange dread filled my heart. This is the one place I never wanted to go. I'm condensing a very long and wonderful story, but that trip to India was one of the greatest adventures of my life. We saw healings, deliverances, and hundreds of Hindus swept into the Kingdom of God. After flying more than thirty hours from Calcutta, India, back to my home in California, I turned around nine days later and flew back. On my second trip, I met a young worship leader[22] whom I have mentored and partnered with for the last decade and a half. My Indian worship leader friend has accelerated to the point where he has led over one million people to Christ through his concerts. Today, India is one of my primary places of passion.

> **We need to test spheres of influence like we judge any part of a prophetic word, but we also need to stay open to the possibility that God is speaking to some hidden treasure within.**

The moral of this story is that it is important to judge your words, but fear should not be allowed to block the focus of your faith. It's true that I should resonate at some point with any prophetic direction that is spoken over me, but I should also keep my heart open to potential blind spots my prophetic words may be revealing. God knew that I had a great calling and destiny in India, so He kindly jumped over my fears to expose me to something good. We need to test spheres of influence like we judge any part of a prophetic word, but we also need to stay open to the possibility that God is speaking to some hidden treasure within us.

No Spheres

By now, some of you may be wondering what to do if your prophetic words did not reveal any spheres of influence. First off, don't be concerned. Not every prophetic word will contain these types of directive descriptors.

Prophetic words are not the only way to determine our spheres of influence. Look back over your history to identify places and people groups where you have demonstrated an unusual level of grace, gifting, favor, influence, or authority. These places may be an indicator of spheres of influence.

---

[22] Allen Ganta, of Hyderabad, India, leads Sounds of the Nations India.

Sometimes prophetic words contain directive material that awakens us to a new area of gifting, identity, calling, or assignment. At other times, prophetic words merely confirm and affirm things that God has already revealed to us. If you discover a sphere of influence through observation of a grace on your life, chances are that it will be confirmed in a prophetic word at some time in the future. However, you don't always need a prophetic word to tell you what to do.

Converging Spheres

Your spheres of influence are not necessarily limited to a single sphere. When processing my sample words, you might have noticed that I have both a geographic and sociographic sphere. I have a call to nations (geographic), and I have a call to worship leaders (sociographic). Each of these spheres of influence are sweet spots for me that I greatly enjoy. But the cross-section between the two spheres holds an even greater level of power, authority, influence, and favor. When I am working with worship leaders in other nations, it seems that every grace and gift I possess is lifted to another level. This happens because it is a cross-section or convergence between two or more spheres of influence. In Scripture, this converging of spheres is called "where the paths meet."[23]

Knowing your spheres of influence helps you know where to fight, who you are fighting alongside of, or who you are fighting for.

Knowing your spheres of influence helps you know where to fight, who you are fighting alongside of, or who you are fighting for. This knowledge often will also tell you what your fight is all about. This information gives your life a strength of focus and direction that empowers you to fight the Good Fight of faith and not just box the air.

---

[23] See Prov 8:1-3.

"WARRING WITH SPHERES OF INFLUENCE" WORKSHEET

1. What spheres of influence appeared within your prophetic words?

_____

_____

_____

2. Were any of these a surprise to you? If so, which ones, and why?

_____

_____

_____

3. Is there any evidence of these spheres in your history? Recount some things from your past that would confirm this sphere of influence for you.

_____

_____

_____

_____

_____

Don't make assumptions about what
God is saying. Ask Him, and be patient
while you wait for the answers.

PROCESSINGSYMBOLS TYPESANDMETAPHORS

J esus presented His message to the people in parables.

Jesus spoke all these things to the crowd in parables; he did not say anything to them without using a parable. So was fulfilled what was spoken through the prophet: "I will open my mouth in parables, I will utter things hidden since the creation of the world."

Matthew 13:34-35

Through the Lord's use of parables, we know that symbolic language is one of the ways God speaks. Because prophetic words are God speaking through people, we find them filled with symbols, types, and metaphors. God is so committed to symbolic language that He used this pictorial realm of types and metaphors to train His Old Testament prophets. To the young prophet Jeremiah God asked, "What do you see?" Jeremiah answered that he saw an almond tree. Then the Lord went on to explain that what Jeremiah had seen spoke of the Lord watching to see that His word was fulfilled. The Father asked again, "What do you see?" Jeremiah answered that he saw a boiling pot. The Lord explained the meaning of the image that Jeremiah saw.[24] This is the same method God used for training the prophets Amos and Zechariah.

---

[24] See Jeremiah chapter one.

God speaks through the known world into the unknown. He parallels things that we understand in the natural realm with things that would normally transcend our comprehension in the spiritual dimension. This is the patience, love, and grace of God to share with each person on a level he or she can understand—the natural realm revealing the spiritual one.

Through the use of parables, we know that symbolic language is one of the ways God speaks.

The book of Romans explains how God reveals spiritual truth through representations in the natural realm.

For since the creation of the world God's invisible qualities—his eternal power and divine nature—have been clearly seen, being understood from what has been made, so that people are without excuse.

Romans 1:20

Recognizing that God speaks to us in this way, one of the prophetic processing tasks is to identify symbolic language and then to formulate questions that lead to deeper understanding of what the Lord is speaking. To identify symbolic language, we should understand that symbols, types, and metaphors can be biblical, topical, or contemporary.

Biblical Symbols, Types, and Metaphors

Biblical types are persons, places, things, actions, or events referred to in Scripture. Anything that appears in your prophetic word that also has a root in Scripture may be revealing a deeper meaning. Biblical prophecies even use symbols, types, and metaphors from other parts of the Bible. For instance, Jesus used the types of Abraham, Noah, Jonah, David, and many other Bible characters to uncover deeper meanings. He also used places like Babylon, Israel, Nineveh, and specific mountains in prophecy. The following passage gives an example of both names and places.

> *A wicked and adulterous generation asks for a sign! But none will be given it except the sign of the prophet Jonah. For as Jonah was three days and three nights in the belly of a huge fish, so the Son of Man will be three days and three nights in the heart of the earth. The men of Nineveh will stand up at the judgment with this generation and condemn it; for they repented at the preaching of Jonah, and now something greater than Jonah is here. The Queen of the South will rise at the judgment with this generation and condemn it; for she came from the ends of the earth to listen to Solomon's wisdom, and now something greater than Solomon is here.*
>
> Matthew 12:39-42

This prophetic word will have much deeper meaning if you know and understand the biblical accounts of Jonah, Nineveh, the Queen of the South, and Solomon. Jesus was speaking to a religious audience that claimed to follow every word of Scripture, so He used biblical types in the form of persons, places, and events they were familiar with to weave even deeper meaning into the words He chose.

In Sample One, the prophet speaks about "restoring the Levitical priesthood of Asaph." Having been to Bible college, and having studied the Word for years, I know who Asaph is. But here is where we want to be careful. Never assume that what you already know about a symbol, type, or metaphor is what God is saying. Be diligent to dialogue with the Lord asking questions like, "In what ways do you want to restore the priesthood of Asaph?" Obviously, God does not want to restore a Levitical system of animal sacrifice. In this case, God was speaking symbolically about raising up a prophetic generation that would train sons and daughters to capture prophetic words in song. Remember that we first identify the symbolic language; then we begin to ask questions that reveal the deeper meaning of what God is speaking.

Anything that appears in your prophetic word that also has a root in Scripture may be revealing a deeper meaning.

Topical Symbols, Types, and Metaphors

Topical symbolic types refer to anything within the created realm. These types include things like trees, plants, animals, colors, vocations, places, household items, tools—the list is endless. In past prophetic words, I have been compared to topical types of a shoe, a hammer, dynamite, an oak tree, a master craftsman, and many more, including the children's toy Mr. Potato Head. Each of these topical types holds a treasure of meaning awaiting deeper research and dialogue. For instance, Jesus used a metaphoric symbol when prophesying over Peter. He compared him to a rock and said:

Upon this rock I will build my church; and the gates of hell shall not prevail against it.

Matthew 16:18b, KJV

He prophetically compared His own relationship to Jerusalem to a mother hen wanting to gather her little chicks under her wings. There are many biblical examples of God using topical symbols, types, and metaphors to prophesy.

Contemporary Symbols, Types, and Metaphors

Contemporary symbols are usually people, places, events, or things appearing as influencers in current society. Contemporary symbolic person types might include a business icon, a government leader, an artist or entertainer, or a religious figure. For instance, I've processed many people's prophetic words that said something like, "You have a Heidi Baker anointing." That comparison could mean many things. Heidi is a woman who cares for the needs of many thousands of orphans in Africa every day. She has seen great healing miracles and even the dead raised. Her ministry motto is, "Stop for the one." The symbolic mention of Heidi Baker is so multifaceted that it is important to ask Holy Spirit questions about what aspect is being highlighted. Does it have to do with Africa? With orphans? With faith? With miracles? With sacrifice? Don't make assumptions about what God is saying. Ask Him, and be patient while you wait for the answers that will increase your understanding.

Jesus prophetically described Himself and John the Baptist as flute players at special occasions. "We played our pipes for you but you wouldn't dance…" In so doing, He compared Himself to contemporary musicians of His day.

Remember that we first identify the symbolic language; then we begin to ask questions that reveal the deeper meaning of what God is speaking.

Our Sample Two says that I would no longer be known as the "town drunk." That is a symbolic type speaking to a seven-year season I had been through of being undone by the strong presence of Holy Spirit. That seven-year experience for me was similar to what the disciples must have experienced on the day of Pentecost when they were accused of being drunk. The day after receiving this word, something definitely changed. I could still access the same joy and awareness of God's presence, but I was no longer totally undone by the experience. The prophetic word was a catalyst for releasing and understanding a new season in my life.

"PROCESSING SYMBOLS, TYPES, AND METAPHORS" PRACTICE

Now that you've seen some examples of symbols, types, and metaphors from Scripture and from my own prophetic words, it's time to practice.

STEP ONE:

Place an asterisk (*) by any word that might be a symbol, type, or metaphor. I have marked Sample One for you as an example.

Sample One

Lord, I bless Your *minstrel prophet in the name of Jesus, who will be used—has been used and will be used—in an international manner to help restore the *tribe of Asaph in the earth. I bless him in the name of the Lord.

We are all *general practitioners, but God gives us *specialty grace. I acknowledge that the Lord has set you into the Body as one of the *Asaphs that raises up the prophetic *Levitical priests to set them in divine order so as to call forth a new sound.

And as the new sound comes forth, heaven responds to the sound of earth. When heaven responds to the sound of earth, heaven comes down and joins in the sound of earth. Then it becomes not only our praises ascending, but heaven has just descended into the earth realm.

So you are called as a *culture creator and an *atmospheric changer to help restore the Asaph priesthood of prophetic order. In Jesus' name. Amen.

Find the remaining symbols, types, and metaphors in Samples Two and Three.

Sample Two

Last night I was praying for you, Dano, and the Lord told me that you are no longer going to be known as the town drunk. Because you've gone through a season of being foolish for God, and now you are going to confound the wise.

And yeah, a change in season—literally with your identity—there is a piece of your identity that you are leaving, and you are coming into a wise thing. I saw the Lord put a helmet on your head, and it said "wisdom" across the top of it. I feel like there is incredible strategic wisdom for the nations.

I feel like you are no longer going to be known for the foolishness—and I mean the foolishness we have when we follow God—but you are going to be known for your wisdom. So you have to take off that first season that the Lord had you in and put this one on. In Jesus' name. Amen.

Sample Three

Hundreds of thousands of dollars. Hundreds of thousands of dollars. Hundreds of thousands of dollars. Hundreds of thousands of dollars. The Lord says, too, that music companies and music stores are going to give you instruments. Music stores are going to give you instruments.

The Lord says that which you are birthing of worship in the earth will be the leading edge of an evangelistic move in the countries that you are working in. You will see your sons filling stadiums. Filling them. Filling them. Filling them. You are already starting to see it. Filling stadiums. For the Lord says it is going to increase because there is a quickening spirit upon you.

The Lord says of that which He has birthed in you, He says breathe on your sons even as Jesus breathed on His disciples and sent them. Breathe on your sons. Breathe on them. Because there is a quickening spirit. And the Lord says they don't have to know everything you know for there is a quickening spirit upon them because God is saying that they have to be accelerated. You see that in the spirit yourself. You see it in the spirit yourself.

For the Lord says there are more nations in His heart for you than what you are seeing right now. More nations in His heart for you. He is going to give you sons. I can see right now a dozen nations that God has given you sons in.

He says hundreds of thousands of dollars are going to come to you. He says ask Me. Ask Me. Ask Me for property; the answer is "yes." Ask Me for recording studios; the answer is "yes" because your sons will become fathers themselves in the anointing that God has given you.

The Lord says that He gives you a quickening spirit. The reason He wants you to breathe on your sons is so that they can go back and become fathers right quick because this is a move that is going to gather pace. It's going to gather pace. Gather pace. It is going to be like a rock rolling down a hill. It is going to go fast. It is going to go fast. So the Lord says great favor is in front of you. A huge wide open space is in front of you. Explore it!

STEP TWO:

Make a list of the symbols, types, and metaphors you found.

- Minstrel prophet
- Asaph
- General Practitioner
- Specialists
- Levitical Priests
- Culture Creators
- Atmospheric Changers
- _____
- _____

STEP THREE:

Formulate questions for research, meditation, and prayer based on your list.

- What is a minstrel prophet?
- What do they do?
- How am I like one?
- Who was Asaph?
- How did he raise up the Levitical priesthood?
- How did he call forth a new sound?
- How does what he did relate to me?
- How does a general practitioner differ from a specialist?

- In what way am I a specialist?
- In what way am I a culture creator?
- Who are some culture creators I should study?
- How is culture created?
- What is an atmospheric changer?
- How is an atmosphere changed?
- What are some things that change atmospheres?
- How do these things relate to me?

_____

_____

_____

_____

Using the following worksheet, take some time to focus on the symbols, types, and metaphors in your own prophetic words.

"PROCESSING SYMBOLS, TYPES, AND METAPHORS" WORKSHEET

STEP ONE:

Place an asterisk (*) by any words in your own prophecies that might be symbolic, types, or metaphors.

STEP TWO:

Make a list of your symbols, types, and metaphors.

_____

_____

_____

_____

_____

_____

_____

STEP THREE:

Formulate questions for research, meditation, and prayer based on your list.

_____

_____

_____

_____

_____

_____

_____

NOTES

_____

_____

_____

_____

_____

_____

Inquiring of the lord is a key to warring
with symbols, types, and metaphors.

WARRING WITH SYMBOLS TYPES AND METAPHORS

A good fight requires good intel—a supply of current and accurate information. We see a biblical basis for symbols, types, and metaphors being one of the ways that God reveals current and accurate information. Yet, because it arrives in this more emblematic form, it requires a different type of processing. Symbols are somewhat subjective in that they can mean different things to different people, so properly warring with your symbols, types, and metaphors involves three disciplines: inquiry, research, and application. Let's look at each of these more closely.

Inquiry

In Old Testament times, kings and elders sought out prophets to "inquire of the Lord." This phrase is used more than a dozen times in the Old Testament in reference to leaders who were asking the Lord's wisdom and counsel through a prophet.[25] The ability to inquire of the Lord stands as one skill every prophetic person should seek to develop. Inquiry is the art of asking great questions then listening for and interacting with God's progressive unveiling of truth.

---

[25] See 1 Kings 22:8, 2 Kings 3:11, and 2 Chron 18:7 for a few examples.

Think of Moses' conversation with God at the burning bush in Exodus chapter three. Moses sees the prophetic sign of a bush that is burning but not consumed. He first turns aside to ask the obvious question, "Why is the bush not burnt?" When God sees Moses turn aside, He begins to speak to him about the call to deliver His people from slavery in Egypt.

Increased knowledge gives way to revelation; revelation births understanding; understanding allows you to act in wisdom.

Then Moses asks, "Who am I, that I should go to Pharaoh, and that I should bring forth the children of Israel out of Egypt?" But God promises to be with Moses.

Then Moses asks, "Who shall I say has sent me?" God gives him the "I AM" revelation.

Moses proceeds to ask, "What if they don't believe me?" The Lord encourages His servant, but Moses presses on to ask, "Can someone else do it?"

In Moses' dialogue with God at the burning bush, you can see the progression of both revelation and inquiry. As God answers one question, a new one forms in response to God's answer. This back-and-forth dialogue between you and Holy Spirit is what we call inquiring of the Lord. In this type of inquiry, new questions form out of what God progressively reveals.

Research

In addition to the art of inquiry, warring with your words requires research. Research is a key for deeper understanding. If the Lord says through a prophetic word that you are like a giant redwood tree, then you will want to study about giant redwood trees. Read books, watch documentaries, perform online searches and find out everything you can about redwood trees. You might find through study that these massive trees can only survive in community with other giant trees. Through this new information you realize that God is speaking to your need or value for community. The point is that while you study, you will gain knowledge that will lead to more spiritual revelation.

Inquiry is the art of asking great questions then listening for and interacting with God's progressive unveiling of truth.

The same is true of a contemporary symbol, type, or metaphor. If God is comparing you to a contemporary figure, then look for a biography or follow articles about him or her. Study interviews, speeches, writings—anything you can get—about the person whom God says you are like. As you are learning and taking in all this information, dialogue with God to gain a more specific understanding about what He is saying to you through this comparison. Increased knowledge gives way to revelation; revelation births understanding; understanding allows you to act in wisdom.

Research gives your initial revelation a root system. A root system allows a plant or tree to endure hardship and tests. It's likely that your word will be tested in the course of this Good Fight. Your revelation roots will help you stand the tests and challenges associated with your promises. The strength of the root system will also ultimately determine how much lasting fruit a plant will bear. Give God-encounters or prophetic revelation a good root system of wisdom, understanding, and knowledge. This practice will ultimately increase the depth of your revelation, the ability to stand strong in times of testing, and expand your capacity to bear fruit in keeping with your prophetic words. This is how we fight the Good Fight.

Application

Another key to warring with prophetic symbols, types, and metaphors is applying what you have learned. The application requires as much wisdom as the interpretation because of its subjective nature. Consider the meaning of an objective/subjective perspective:

We don't assume that everything we learn applies to what God is saying, so we study from a place of communion.

> *An objective perspective is one that is not influenced by emotions, opinions, or personal feelings—it is a perspective based in fact, in things quantifiable and measurable. A subjective perspective is one open to greater interpretation based on personal feeling, emotion, aesthetics, etc. . . . For example, I may take an objective perspective that the Bible is the most published book in all of history. This can be verified as a factual statement by looking at publishing records and statistics. A subjective view would state that the Bible is the most influential book of all time or that is the greatest book of all time. I cannot verify these statements with fact—only through opinion.*[26]

---

[26] Sourced from www.quora.com, "differences between objective and subjective."

Remember the Heidi Baker illustration in the last chapter? The word said, "You have an anointing like Heidi Baker." It would not be wise to immediately assume that the Heidi Baker similarity meant you should quit your job and move to Africa. The application is as important as the inspiration. Remembering that all prophetic words are partial[27] and require judging[28] is part of fighting the Good Fight.

In the book of Daniel, we have a classic example of misapplication of a proper prophetic encounter and interpretation. The king has a prophetic dream, and he uses the opportunity to test the accuracy of his spiritual counselors. He tells no one the dream but demands that the magicians, enchanters, sorcerers, and astrologers tell him both what he dreamed as well as the interpretation of the dream. The spiritual community was outraged! They responded to the king:

> *There is no one on earth who can do what the king asks! No king, however great and mighty, has ever asked such a thing of any magician or enchanter or astrologer.*
>
> Daniel 2:10

But Daniel, by the Spirit of God, was given the word of knowledge to reveal the king's dream and the prophetic interpretation of what it meant. In his dream, the king saw a statue with a head of gold. Daniel explained:

Properly warring with your symbols, types, and metaphors involves three disciplines: inquiry, research, and application.

> *Your Majesty, you are the king of kings. The God of heaven has given you dominion and power and might and glory. . . . You are the head of gold.*
>
> vs 37-38

After Daniel's prophetic interpretation of the dream, it seems all has gone well for him and his three Hebrew peers, Shadrach, Meshach, and Abednego. Daniel's friends were promoted as administrators over the province of Babylon, and Daniel was highly honored serving in the royal court.

However, the next chapter opens with the phrase:

---

[27] 1 Cor 13:9.
[28] 1 Cor 14:29.

King Nebuchadnezzar made an image of gold, sixty cubits high and six cubits wide, and set it up on the plain of Dura in the province of Babylon.

3:1

The king declared that anyone who did not worship the image would be thrown into a blazing furnace. Because the Hebrews wouldn't bow to the image, they went straight from promotion to almost being incinerated. Wow! Let's talk about misapplying a prophetic symbol. The prophetic word was right; the interpretation was right; but the application was disastrous.

On the day of Pentecost, God released a prophetic symbol as the disciples spoke supernaturally in the tongues of every nation under heaven. This prophetic sign caused the crowd to ask, "What does this mean?"[29] Peter stood among them and began to explain that what they were experiencing was the fulfillment of a word spoken by the prophet Joel and a sign of the resurrection of Jesus Christ. This answer inspired a new question, "What shall we do?"[30] In regards to symbolic language, it is important to not only ask, "What does this mean?" but also to inquire, "Lord, what should we do?" This is the discipline of seeking a wise application.

---

[29] Acts 2:12.
[30] v 37.

"WARRING WITH SYMBOLS, TYPES, AND METAPHORS" WORKSHEET

Inquiry

Take one of your symbols, types, or metaphors and begin to inquire of the Lord. Ask Him, "What does this mean?" Write down the perceptions you receive. God speaking to you may come as a picture, a thought, an imagination, a feeling, an impression, an idea, a memory, or a revelation. Ask additional questions until the meaning of what God is speaking becomes clear to you.

_____

_____

_____

Research

Use books, encyclopedias, online searches, articles, documentaries, and, of course, the Bible to research deeper into understanding what God is speaking. Proverbs 25:2 says:

> It is the glory of God to conceal a matter; to search out a matter is the glory of kings.

I believe you will experience greater levels of God's glory as you dig deeper into knowing and understanding the depth behind prophetic symbols. The research stage is still a dialogue. Don't assume that everything you learn applies to what God is saying. We study from a place of communion. We seek; God speaks.

> The heart of the discerning acquires knowledge, for the ears of the wise seek it out.

> Proverbs 18:15

Seek knowledge with your heart, and listen for wisdom.

Application

It's time to ask the follow-up question asked by the crowd at Pentecost, [31] "What should we do?" With all that has been revealed through your inquiry and research, how should you move forward?

_____

_____

_____

I advise seeking some counsel on this one. Since judging prophecy is meant to be done in community and plans fail for lack of counsel, wisdom dictates a team approach. It may be time to consult with a few loved ones and leaders about what the Lord has said and what their counsel would be on how to respond.

> *Wisdom is found in those who take advice.*
>
> Proverbs 13:10

Wage war with the counsel of others. This is the Good Fight.

NOTES

_____

_____

_____

_____

_____

---

[31] See Acts 2:37.

Studying major and minor themes within
your prophetic words will help you
align with your top priorities and
establish your highest intentions.

PROCESSING**MAJOR**AND **MINOR**THEMES

Our final processing step is a safeguard to make sure you are focusing your attention on the most important aspects of what God is saying. With all the processing steps I've given you, it would be easy to get lost down the rabbit hole of chasing the minutiae of every detail or image in your prophetic words. Studying major and minor themes within your prophetic words will help you align with your top priorities and establish your highest intentions.

We identify major or minor themes through noting repetition within the prophecy. Repeated ideas or words are indicators that something is important. We will talk more about this in the next chapter.

For now, let's get right to it. This processing step is simple, but its ability to clarify focus is powerful. Let's practice finding major and minor themes first in Sample Three.

"PROCESSING MAJOR AND MINOR THEMES" PRACTICE

STEP ONE:

Look through Sample Three for any words or ideas that are repeated. Include also words or ideas that would be synonyms of the repeated word. In the example, I highlighted the repeated word and added a superscript to indicate the number of times that word or idea has appeared throughout the prophecy. I have begun Sample Three for you by marking two different repeated words ("sons" and "quickening spirit"). Your first practice assignment is to mark any other repeated words you find in Sample Three.

Sample Three

Hundreds of thousands of dollars. Hundreds of thousands of dollars. Hundreds of thousands of dollars. Hundreds of thousands of dollars. The Lord says, too, that music companies and music stores are going to give you instruments. Music stores are going to give you instruments.

The Lord says that which you are birthing of worship in the earth will be the leading edge of an evangelistic move in the countries that you are working in. You will see your sons[1] filling stadiums. Filling them. Filling them. Filling them. You are already starting to see it. Filling stadiums. For the Lord says it is going to increase because there is a quickening spirit[1] upon you.

The Lord says of that which He has birthed in you, He says breathe on your sons[2] even as Jesus breathed on His disciples and sent them. Breathe on your sons[3]. Breathe on them[4]. Because there is a quickening spirit[2]. And the Lord says they[5] don't have to know everything you know for there is a quickening spirit[3] upon them[6] because God is saying that they[7] have to be accelerated[4]. You see that in the spirit yourself. You see it in the spirit yourself.

For the Lord says there are more nations in His heart for you than what you are seeing right now. More nations in His heart for you. He is going to give you sons[8]. I can see right now a dozen nations that God has given you sons[9] in.

He says hundreds of thousands of dollars are going to come to you. He says ask Me. Ask Me. Ask Me for property; the answer is "yes." Ask Me for recording studios; the answer is "yes" because your sons[10] will become fathers themselves in the anointing that God has given you.

The Lord says that He gives you a quickening spirit[5]. The reason He wants you to breathe on your sons[11] is so that they can go back and become fathers right quick[6] because this is a move that is going to gather pace[7]. It's going to gather pace[8]. Gather pace[9]. It is going to be like a rock rolling down a hill[10]. It is going to go fast[11]. It is going to go fast[12]. So the Lord says great favor is in front of you. A huge wide open space is in front of you. Explore it!

STEP TWO:

Make a table of major themes you found in Sample Three.

# Of Times Repeated	Repeated Words, Ideas, or Phrases
12	quickening spirit, quicken, gather pace, go fast
12	sons, they, them

STEP THREE:

Now do the same for Samples One and Two. Add their major themes to the charts below. Where you find major themes that show up in two or more prophecies, mark them and continue numbering from where you last left off, resulting in an end count of the number of times that word was repeated across all three samples.

Sample One

Lord, I bless Your minstrel prophet in the Name of Jesus, who will be used—has been used and will be used—in an international manner to help restore the tribe of Asaph in the earth. I bless him in the Name of the Lord.

We are all general practitioners, but God gives us specialty grace. I acknowledge that the Lord has set you into the Body as one of the Asaphs that raises up the prophetic Levitical priests to set them in divine order so as to call forth a new sound.

And as the new sound comes forth, heaven responds to the sound of earth. When heaven responds to the sound of earth, heaven comes down and joins in the sound of earth. Then it becomes not only our praises ascending, but heaven has just descended into the earth realm.

So you are called as a culture creator, and an atmospheric changer to help restore the Asaph priesthood of prophetic order in Jesus' name. Amen.

Sample Two

Last night I was praying for you, Dano, and the Lord told me that you are no longer going to be known as the town drunk. Because you've gone through a season of being foolish for God, and now you are going to confound the wise.

And yeah, a change in season—literally with your identity—there is a piece of your identity that you are leaving, and you are coming into a wise thing. I saw the Lord put a helmet on your head, and it said "wisdom" across the top of it. I feel like there is incredible strategic wisdom for the nations.

I feel like you are no longer going to be known for the foolishness—and I mean the foolishness we have when we follow God—but you are going to be known for your wisdom. So you have to take off that first season that the Lord had you in and put this one on. In Jesus' name. Amen.

Samples One and Two Major Themes

# Of Times Repeated	Repeated Words, Ideas, or Phrases

In comparing Samples One and Two to the first one we practiced, you should have found a few similarities in the areas of sounds, nations, and worship. Therefore, the recipient of these words should focus intentional attention on what God is saying to him regarding these things. Their repetition marks them as important.

"PROCESSING MAJOR AND MINOR THEMES" WORKSHEET

STEP ONE:

Look through one of your personal prophecies for any words or ideas that are repeated. Include words or ideas that are synonyms of the repeated word. Mark or highlight each repeated word and add a superscript to indicate the number of times that word or idea appears throughout the prophecy.

STEP TWO:

Use the table below to record repeated words, ideas, and phrases you highlighted.

Samples One and Two Major Themes

# Of Times Repeated	Repeated Words, Ideas, or Phrases

STEP THREE:

Now do the same for any other of your personal prophecies you are processing at the same time. Add their major themes to the chart. When you find major themes that show up in two or more prophecies, continue numbering from where you last left off. Your end result will be a total count of the number of times that word was repeated across all the prophecies you are working with.

NOTES

_____

_____

_____

_____

_____

_____

_____

_____

_____

_____

We fight the Good Fight by focusing on
the major themes God is speaking to.

15

WARRING WITH MAJOR AND MINOR THEMES

God uses repetition for accountability and confirmation. Throughout Scripture, we find the principle of verifying something important through the testimony of two or three witnesses. Look at the following examples:

- **In matters of wrongdoing**: "By the testimony of two or three witnesses" (Matt 18:16).

- **In prayer:** "If two of you on earth agree about anything they ask for, it will be done for them by my Father in heaven" (Matt 18:19).

- **In prophetic protocol**: "Two or three prophets should speak, and the others should weigh carefully what is said" (1 Cor 14:29).

- **In every matter:** "Every matter must be established by the testimony of two or three witnesses" (2 Cor 13:1).

This principle forms the basis for why we do prophetic processing with more than one prophetic word. Repetition within a single word is significant and important, but when you receive the same types of words from different people with the added variables of location and occasion, then it should certainly be considered more seriously than the weight a single word carries. I'm not saying that a word cannot stand alone as the word of the Lord or that you must wait for verification from other prophetic words or voices. I'm emphasizing that if God has said the same thing to you on multiple occasions through multiple voices, you may want to take notice.

Verification

As we said earlier, sometimes God uses repetition for verification or emphasis. He repeats things in a word or through a series of words to emphasize how important this issue is. Twenty-five times in John's gospel, Jesus started a sentence with the words, "Verily, verily, I say unto you." The word in the Greek language is actually "amen." In this repetition of the words, "verily, verily," Jesus demonstrated the importance of what He was about to say. The same is true for words that are repeated within your prophetic words. Repetition occurs for emphasis and verification of major themes.

> **If God has said the same thing to you on multiple occasions, through multiple voices, you may want to take notice.**

Warning

Repetition can also serve as a warning that you are not listening or not acting on your prophetic words. I've met people whom after receiving a prophetic encouragement from me said, "Oh yes, I've received that word a dozen times." I immediately ask, "Well, what are you doing about it?"

God cries through the prophet Jeremiah and others:

> *"For they have not listened to my words," declares the LORD, "words that I sent to them again and again by my servants the prophets. And you exiles have not listened either," declares the LORD.*

> 29:19

I don't think we want to be found in this category, but unfortunately it does happen. The failure to act on or believe a prophetic word can cause it to surface again and again. This may be God pleading for your attention . . . and action.

Majoring On Minors

Another reason we do this major and minor theme exercise is to make sure we are not majoring on minors. Sometimes we are drawn to the part of a prophetic word we are most excited about and ignore the rest. That is particularly dangerous when that idea or theme is only mentioned one time and other themes are screaming to be heard.

In our practice samples, you can see that some of the major themes are actions. "Ask" is repeated several times, as is "breathe on." The amount of repetition is supporting the importance of my need for action in those specific areas. By recognizing the repetition of the dozen references to "sons" in Sample Three, it appears that I should be more focused on my spiritual sons than I am even upon myself. That is an important life emphasis. Taking time to process the number of repetitions in your prophetic words can help you sort what are the primary and secondary things God is speaking to you in order to fight the Good Fight.

Divine Meaning of Numbers

Throughout Scripture, the use of numbers within God's messages given through His prophets had deep and significant meaning. God often speaks symbolically through the use of numbering. He may be speaking to you through how many times something is mentioned in your prophetic words. You may have also experienced a specific number—or numbers—repeated in various ways in your life.

> **Sometimes we are drawn to the part of a prophetic word that we are most excited about and ignore the rest. Make sure you are not majoring on minors.**

"Numerology" can be defined as "ascribing divine meaning to a number or its usage." I know this is a term that has primarily been used outside of Christianity, but because I believe Christ has redeemed everything in creation and restored all to the glory and honor of God, I believe God continues to speak symbolically through numbers.

I remember processing with one of our students three of her prophetic words, which together contained the word "breakthrough" twenty-one times. It's interesting to note that the number twenty-one is often symbolic of breakthrough. Could this be more than a coincidence? Without getting too spooky about it, I truly believe it can. Those twenty-one references were across three different words, spoken at various times, and delivered in diverse locations by distinctive speakers. God does not waste words; He is very precise. I have often seen "grace" spoken five times—five being a number associated with grace. Eleven is one number which represents new beginnings, and I have seen promises of a "new thing" or "new season" listed eleven times.

Though you may not quite understand or even appreciate the idea of prophetic numerology in order to process your major and minor themes, I want to encourage you to ask the Holy Spirit if He is speaking something personally significant through the numbers of repetition within your words.

"WARRING WITH MAJOR AND MINOR THEMES" WORKSHEET

1. Review the words you have listed in your major and minor theme table from the preceding chapter's assignment. Are you surprised by any of the words presenting as major themes? Ask yourself whether you have been treating this subject as a major theme in your life? What would it look like to do so?

_____

_____

_____

2. I remember a season where I felt pressured to take the senior leader position of a church that I served because I thought it was a major theme within my prophetic words. When I reviewed carefully my major and minor themes, that idea only appeared one time within the content of more than fifty prophetic words. Realizing that this was not a major theme helped me to get back on track with things God was truly indicating as primary.

Are there any minor themes in your prophetic words that you have been overemphasizing? How does what you are currently pursuing align or not align with the major and minor themes of your prophetic words? What do you think you should do if you find that you are majoring on something that is presenting within your prophetic words as a minor theme?

_____

_____

_____

_____

3. Are you one of those persons who has had the same word spoken over you time and time again? How well do you believe you have agreed with, aligned with, and appropriated the major themes of those repeated words? What might be some steps you could take to increase your synergy with what God is repeatedly saying?

_____

_____

_____

4. Do you believe the number of times a subject is listed has any spiritual significance? If so, what additional information or confirmations might be present through the quantity of repetition of major themes in your prophetic words?

_____

_____

_____

NOTES

Prophetic processing is not a one-time event but rather entering into a long-term relationship with your prophetic words.

YOUR**GOOD**FIGHT

A good fight is one that you win. The tools in this workbook are weapons for sustaining and advancing your victory. Let's revisit each of the goals we presented in the Introduction:

- Discover who you are as a new creation in Christ Jesus.

- Stand on what God has promised He will do for you.

- Know what you can do to agree, align, and appropriate God's intentions towards you.

- Identify mindsets, cautions, and actions that will accelerate the fulfillment of promises.

- Possess a clearer understanding of your assigned spheres of influence.

- Properly discern your times and seasons to stay in rest and strength.

- Unpack the deeper meanings behind symbols, types, and metaphors.

- Identify major and minor themes to properly align with God's priorities for you.

Through the tools I have presented, you can see that prophetic processing is not a one-time event but rather more like entering into a long-term relationship with your prophetic words. The more you interact with your prophetic words, the more they will speak to you and pour forth their grace of strength, courage, and comfort.

A good fight is one you win.

I hope you have achieved at least one of our initial goals by processing through this workbook. Each tool and technique is like a new weapon in your arsenal for fighting the Good Fight of faith with the prophetic words spoken over you.

In the remainder of this chapter, I would like to ask a series of questions that relate to each of the tools or weapons you have learned in this workbook. Your answers and recall will show where you are in internalizing what you have learned through your prophetic processing journey. If you don't have a clear answer to one of the following questions, consider returning to the chapter it relates to and work on mastering that tool.

Remember that the Good Fight is the one that you **win**, and to the victor go the spoils.

"YOUR GOOD FIGHT" WORKSHEET

Discover Who You Are

From memory, write the "I Am" statement you created using the identity statements present in your prophetic words.

_____

_____

_____

_____

If you don't have your "I Am" statement memorized yet, work on committing it to memory. You may want to create a short version and an expanded version of your heavenly identity statement, committing the shorter version to memory. Never forget that your heavenly identity is the primary place you fight from. Who God says you are is the truest thing in the universe about you. Whenever your feelings, attitudes, thoughts, or behaviors fail to represent who God says you are, then reposition yourself. Step into your heavenly identity and the favor, authority, and influence it offers you as a child of God. This is your core position for fighting the Good Fight.

Agree, Align, Appropriate

What alignment steps have you taken in order to agree with what God says about you? What things do you need to take off and what things are you putting on? What is your next step in appropriating the favor and authority God has promised you?

_____

_____

_____

Stand on the Promises

Write out in the space below the things God has promised you that are foremost in your memory. You can't fight the Good Fight with things you do not remember.

_____

_____

_____

_____

_____

If your circumstances look contrary to your promises, then take it as a personal challenge to stay in a place of faith, hope, and expectancy. This is your opportunity to believe purely from faith rather than circumstances. Feel free to challenge your circumstances with a declaration of what God has promised.

Actions that Accelerate

How are you currently positioning yourself to meet the conditions of a specific promise? Is your positioning mainly in the realm of changing a mindset, observing a caution, or taking a specific action?

_____

_____

_____

_____

Keep a record or journal of when you started repositioning yourself and note the changes you see in yourself and your circumstances related to your personal acceleration. This record book will serve as an encouragement and a documentation of the rate of your acceleration as you fight the Good Fight.

Times and Seasons

How would you define your current season?

_____

_____

_____

What are the things you are called to focus on in the present season?

_____

_____

_____

Are you taking time to enjoy the season that you are in?

_____

_____

_____

What preparations do you need to make to step into the next season?

_____

_____

_____

_____

Spheres of Influence

What are the primary spheres of influence that God has assigned to you?

_____

_____

_____

What percentage of your time do you currently spend within your spheres of influence?

_____

What things could you do to get more involved in your spheres of influence?

_____

_____

_____

Symbols, Types, and Metaphors

Which symbol, type, or metaphor are you currently researching?

_____

_____

What is the most significant thing you have learned through your research so far that relates directly to your prophetic word and destiny?

_____

_____

Majors and Minors

What are you doing right now to stay focused on the major themes that God has spoken over you?

_____

_____

_____

NOTES

_____

_____

_____

_____

_____

_____

_____

_____

_____

Appendix I

PROCESSINGWORKSHEETS

PREPARING FOR PROPHETIC PROCESSING

This Appendix will take you through the steps of analyzing and processing prophetic words you have received. Throughout these instructions, I will be using some of my own personal words to illustrate the principles taught and for you to practice the assignments on. However, there are a few things for you to do in preparation before we get started in order for you to get the most out of this process.

STEP ONE:

Transcribe your prophetic words to prepare for processing. Type out your words double-spaced using a large font so you will have plenty of room for notes. At the top of each page, reference who delivered the word, where it was delivered, and the date it was delivered. For example:

John Smith to Dan McCollam
at Really Inspirational Conference
My Town, CA
March, 27, 2017

STEP TWO:

Judge your prophetic words as described earlier in Chapter One before beginning this process. You are free to cross-out, discard, or flush any words that don't fit the criteria we talked about. We want to process only what is good and only what resonates in your spirit as a true word from God.

Here is a brief review of our judging criteria.

1. Does anything in your prophetic words conflict with Scripture or the character and nature of God?

2. Does the one delivering the word have anything to gain or any personal benefit from the potential outcome of the prophetic word?

3. Does the word resonate with you? Is there a sense of internal agreement even if parts of the word challenge you?

4. How do loved ones and leaders around you view this word? Are there any parts of the word they are questioning the validity of?

STEP THREE:

Take two or three prophetic words you have judged to be "God words" for this season and print them out on paper for easier processing.

"PROCESSING IDENTITY" WORKSHEET

Gather two to three of your typed out and printed personal prophetic words. Choose words that you resonate with and which you have already judged as good and from the Lord.

STEP ONE:

Carefully read through your personal prophetic words and circle any obvious statements of identity.

STEP TWO:

Read through your words again, this time circling any implied statements of identity.

STEP THREE:

Make a list of identity statements revealed in steps one and two.

- _____
- _____
- _____
- _____
- _____
- _____

STEP FOUR:

Craft an "I Am . . ." statement of three to five sentences summarizing the highlights of how you are known and seen in heaven.

My "I Am" Statement

I am . . .

_____

_____

_____

_____

"PROCESSING PROMISES" WORKSHEET

STEP ONE:

Using the same words from which you pulled out identity statements, identify promise statements expressing God's intentions towards you and underline them.

STEP TWO:

List God's statements of promise and intention in a list form. Feel free to paraphrase while using caution not to change the meaning of the promise.

- _____
- _____
- _____
- _____

STEP THREE:

Form a crafted prayer of declaration and thanksgiving from God's promises towards you.

Lord, thank You that You have said . . .

_____

_____

_____

_____

_____

"PROCESSING CONDITIONS" WORKSHEET

STEP ONE:

Identify conditional promises, command statements, and principled conditions. Look for words like

> after, as you, as long as, as soon as, assuming that, before, if, if only, in order to, once, only if, provided that, so long as, therefore, unless, until, while you, when, whenever, wherever

Action verbs connected to a specific promise are cues that a conditional command may be present. Draw a rectangle around any of these conditional statements of promise.

STEP TWO:

Put your conditional promises into a table with the required action on one side and the promised outcome on the other.

Action/Outcome Chart

Action	Outcome

STEP THREE:

Create a MAP (Ministry Action Plan) from your listed conditions.

I will _____

I will _____

I will _____

I will _____

"PROCESSING TIMES AND SEASONS" WORKSHEET

STEP ONE:

Put a triangle around any timing words you spot in your prophetic words and note the phrases they are attached to. Here is a list of some common timing words:

after, at hand, at that time, before, coming, day, decade, delay, during, earlier, era, every day, future, hour, in time, later, minute, momentary, now, new, past, present, season, soon, someday, sometime, sunrise, sunset, then, times, today, tomorrow, weeks, when, yesterday

STEP TWO:

Put these timing phrases into a times and seasons graph.

Times and Seasons Graph

Past	Present	Soon	Later

THE GOOD FIGHT

STEP THREE:

Create a declaration of timing for yourself.

I'm no longer . . .

_____

_____

_____

I am now . . .

_____

_____

_____

I will soon . . .

_____

_____

_____

In the future, I will . . .

_____

_____

_____

The Good Fight Copyright © 2017—Dan McCollam

"PROCESSING SPHERES OF INFLUENCE" WORKSHEET

STEP ONE:

Look for any assignment of spheres involving people, places, or special areas of interests within your prophetic words. Underscore them with a dotted line.

STEP TWO:

List the information you underscored in the space provided below.

- _____
- _____
- _____

STEP THREE:

Categorize the information of people, places and interest groups into the spaces below.

Geographic Sphere: Where should I focus my efforts?

_____

_____

Demographic Sphere: Who should I be serving?

_____

_____

Sociographic Sphere: What am I best equipped to do?

_____

_____

"PROCESSING SYMBOLS, TYPES, AND METAPHORS" WORKSHEET

STEP ONE:

Place an asterisk (*) by any words in your own prophecies that might be symbolic, types, or metaphors.

STEP TWO:

Make a list of your symbols, types, and metaphors.

_____

_____

_____

_____

_____

_____

_____

T

STEP THREE:

Formulate questions for research, meditation, and prayer based on your list.

_____

_____

_____

_____

_____

_____

"PROCESSING MAJOR AND MINOR THEMES" WORKSHEET

STEP ONE:

Look through one of your personal prophecies for any words or ideas that are repeated. Include words or ideas that are synonyms of the repeated word. Mark or highlight each repeated word and add a superscript to indicate the number of times that word or idea appears throughout the prophecy.

STEP TWO:

Use the table below to list repeated words, ideas, and phrases you highlighted.

Repeated Words, Ideas, or Phrases

# of Times Repeated	Repeated Words, Ideas, or Phrases

STEP THREE:

Now do the same for any other of your personal prophecies you are processing at the same time. Add their major themes to the chart. When you find major themes that show up in two or more prophecies, continue numbering from where you last left off. Your end result will then be a total count of the number of times that word was repeated across all the prophecies you are working with.

Appendix II

PROCESSING
QUICK**REFERENCE**SHEET

CIRCLE statements of IDENTITY

UNDERLINE statements of SOVEREIGN PROMISE

Draw a RECTANGLE around CONDITIONAL PROMISES and COMMANDS

Place a TRIANGLE around TIMING WORDS

Put an *ASTERISK by SYMBOLS, TYPES, and METAPHORS

UNDERSCORE with a dotted line REFERENCES TO SPHERE OF INFLUENCE

SUPERSCRIPT[1,2,3] the number of times a MAJOR or MINOR THEME appears

Appendix III

SAMPLES
ONE, **TWO,** AND **THREE**
FOR **PRACTICE** PROCESSING

SAMPLEONE

Lord, I bless Your minstrel prophet in the name of Jesus, who will be used—has been used and will be used—in an international manner to help restore the tribe of Asaph in the earth. I bless him in the name of the Lord.

We are all general practitioners, but God gives us specialty grace. I acknowledge that the Lord has set you into the Body as one of the Asaphs that raises up the prophetic Levitical priests to set them in divine order so as to call forth a new sound.

And as the new sound comes forth, heaven responds to the sound of earth. When heaven responds to the sound of earth, heaven comes down and joins in the sound of earth. Then it becomes not only our praises ascending, but heaven has just descended into the earth realm.

So you are called as a culture creator and an atmospheric changer to help restore the Asaph priesthood of prophetic order. In Jesus' name. Amen.

SAMPLE TWO

Last night I was praying for you, Dano, and the Lord told me that you are no longer going to be known as the town drunk. Because you've gone through a season of being foolish for God, and now you are going to confound the wise.

And yeah, a change in season—literally with your identity—there is a piece of your identity that you are leaving, and you are coming into a wise thing. I saw the Lord put a helmet on your head, and it said "wisdom" across the top of it. I feel like there is incredible strategic wisdom for the nations.

I feel like you are no longer going to be known for the foolishness—and I mean the foolishness we have when we follow God—but you are going to be known for your wisdom. So you have to take off that first season that the Lord had you in and put this one on. In Jesus' name. Amen.

SAMPLE THREE

Hundreds of thousands of dollars. Hundreds of thousands of dollars. Hundreds of thousands of dollars. Hundreds of thousands of dollars. The Lord says, too, that music companies and music stores are going to give you instruments. Music stores are going to give you instruments.

The Lord says that which you are birthing of worship in the earth will be the leading edge of an evangelistic move in the countries that you are working in. You will see your sons filling stadiums. Filling them. Filling them. Filling them. You are already starting to see it. Filling stadiums. For the Lord says it is going to increase because there is a quickening spirit upon you.

The Lord says of that which He has birthed in you, He says breathe on your sons even as Jesus breathed on His disciples and sent them. Breathe on your sons. Breathe on them. Because there is a quickening spirit. And the Lord says they don't have to know everything you know for there is a quickening spirit upon them because God is saying that they have to be accelerated. You see that in the spirit yourself. You see it in the spirit yourself.

For the Lord says there are more nations in His heart for you than what you are seeing right now. More nations in His heart for you. He is going to give you sons. I can see right now a dozen nations that God has given you sons in.

He says hundreds of thousands of dollars are going to come to you. He says ask Me. Ask Me. Ask Me for property; the answer is "yes." Ask Me for recording studios; the answer is "yes" because your sons will become fathers themselves in the anointing that God has given you.

The Lord says that He gives you a quickening spirit. The reason He wants you to breathe on your sons is so that they can go back and become fathers right quick because this is a move that is going to gather pace. It's going to gather pace. Gather pace. It is going to be like a rock rolling down a hill. It is going to go fast. It is going to go fast. So the Lord says great favor is in front of you. A huge wide open space is in front of you. Explore it!

Appendix IV

ANSWERKEYS

ANSWER KEY: "PROCESSING IDENTITY" PRACTICE

(Note: This is from Chapter 1.)

STEP ONE:

Circle statements of identity.

Sample One

Lord, I bless Your minstrel prophet in the name of Jesus, who will be used—has been used and will be used—in an international manner to help restore the tribe of Asaph in the earth. I bless him in the name of the Lord.

We are all general practitioners, but God gives us specialty grace. I acknowledge that the Lord has set you into the Body as one of the Asaphs that raises up the prophetic Levitical priests to set them in divine order so as to call forth a new sound.

And as the new sound comes forth, heaven responds to the sound of earth. When heaven responds to the sound of earth, heaven comes down and joins in the sound of earth. Then it becomes not only our praises ascending, but heaven has just descended into the earth realm.

So you are called as a culture creator and an atmospheric changer to help restore the Asaph priesthood of prophetic order. In Jesus' name. Amen.

Now see if you can find any identity statements in Sample Two.

Sample Two

Last night I was praying for you, Dano, and the Lord told me that you are no longer going to be known as the town drunk. Because you've gone through a season of being foolish for God, and now you are going to confound the wise.

And yeah, a change in season—literally with your identity—there is a piece of your identity that you are leaving, and you are coming into a wise thing. I saw the Lord put a helmet on your head, and it said "wisdom" across the top of it. I feel like there is incredible strategic wisdom for the nations.

I feel like you are no longer going to be known for the foolishness—and I mean the foolishness we have when we follow God—but you are going to be known for your wisdom. So you have to take off that first season that the Lord had you in and put this one on. In Jesus' name. Amen.

STEP TWO:

Circle implied statements of identity.

Sample Three

Hundreds of thousands of dollars. Hundreds of thousands of dollars. Hundreds of thousands of dollars. Hundreds of thousands of dollars. The Lord says, too, that music companies and music stores are going to give you instruments. Music stores are going to give you instruments.

The Lord says that which you are birthing of worship in the earth will be the leading edge of an evangelistic move in the countries that you are working in. You will see your sons filling stadiums. Filling them. Filling them. Filling them. You are already starting to see it. Filling stadiums. For the Lord says it is going to increase because there is a quickening spirit upon you.

The Lord says of that which He has birthed in you, He says breathe on your sons even as Jesus breathed on His disciples and sent them. Breathe on your sons. Breathe on them. Because there is a quickening spirit. And the Lord says they don't have to know everything you know for there is a quickening spirit upon them because God is saying that they have to be accelerated. You see that in the spirit yourself. You see it in the spirit yourself.

For the Lord says there are more nations in His heart for you than what you are seeing right now. More nations in His heart for you. He is going to give you sons. I can see right now a dozen nations that God has given you sons in.

He says hundreds of thousands of dollars are going to come to you. He says ask Me. Ask Me. Ask Me for property; the answer is "yes." Ask Me for recording studios; the answer is "yes" because your sons will become fathers themselves in the anointing that God has given you.

The Lord says that He gives you a quickening spirit. The reason He wants you to breathe on your sons is so that they can go back and become fathers right quick because this is a move that is going to gather pace. It's going to gather pace. Gather pace. It is going to be like a rock rolling down a hill. It is going to go fast. It is going to go fast. So the Lord says great favor is in front of you. A huge wide open space is in front of you. Explore it!

STEP THREE:

Make a list of identity statements you highlighted from the sample words, both directly stated and implied.

- Minstrel prophet
- One of the Asaphs
- Culture creator
- Atmospheric changer
- No longer the "town drunk"
- Man of wisdom
- Father to fathers

STEP FOUR:

Create an "I Am" statement.

I am a minstrel prophet restoring the Asaph priesthood in the earth. I am a culture creator and an atmospheric changer. I am a man of strategic wisdom for the nations, a father to fathers and sons who will be the leading edge of evangelistic movements around the world.

ANSWER KEY:
"PROCESSING PROMISE" PRACTICE

(Note: This is from Chapter 4.)

STEP ONE:

Identify promise statements expressing God's intentions towards the recipient and underline them.

Sample Two

Last night I was praying for you, Dano, and the Lord told me that you are no longer going to be known as the town drunk. Because you've gone through a season of being foolish for God, and now you are going to confound the wise.

And yeah, a change in season—literally with your identity—there is a piece of your identity that you are leaving, and you are coming into a wise thing. I saw the Lord put a helmet on your head, and it said "wisdom" across the top of it. I feel like there is incredible strategic wisdom for the nations.

I feel like you are no longer going to be known for the foolishness—and I mean the foolishness we have when we follow God—but you are going to be known for your wisdom. So you have to take off that first season that the Lord had you in and put this one on. In Jesus' name. Amen.

Sample Three

Hundreds of thousands of dollars. Hundreds of thousands of dollars. Hundreds of thousands of dollars. Hundreds of thousands of dollars. The Lord says, too, that music companies and music stores are going to give you instruments. Music stores are going to give you instruments.

The Lord says that which you are birthing of worship in the earth will be the leading edge of an evangelistic move in the countries that you are working in. You will see your sons filling stadiums. Filling them. Filling them. Filling them.

You are already starting to see it. Filling stadiums. For the Lord says it is going to increase because there is a quickening spirit upon you.

The Lord says of that which He has birthed in you, He says breathe on your sons even as Jesus breathed on His disciples and sent them. Breathe on your sons. Breathe on them. Because there is a quickening spirit. And the Lord says they don't have to know everything you know for there is a quickening spirit upon them because God is saying that they have to be accelerated. You see that in the spirit yourself. You see it in the spirit yourself.

For the Lord says there are more nations in His heart for you than what you are seeing right now. More nations in His heart for you. He is going to give you sons. I can see right now a dozen nations that God has given you sons in.

He says hundreds of thousands of dollars are going to come to you. He says ask Me. Ask Me. Ask Me for property; the answer is "yes." Ask Me for recording studios; the answer is "yes" because your sons will become fathers themselves in the anointing that God has given you.

The Lord says that He gives you a quickening spirit. The reason He wants you to breathe on your sons is so that they can go back and become fathers right quick because this is a move that is going to gather pace. It's going to gather pace. Gather pace. It is going to be like a rock rolling down a hill. It is going to go fast. It is going to go fast. So the Lord says great favor is in front of you. A huge wide open space is in front of you. Explore it!

STEP TWO:

List the statements of promise and intention from all three samples in a list form.

- You will help restore the tribe of Asaph in the earth
- You have a specialty grace
- You will call forth the new sound
- Now you are going to confound the wise
- You are coming into a wise thing
- There is strategic wisdom for the nations
- You are going to be known for your wisdom
- Hundreds of thousands of dollars
- Music companies and stores are going to give you instruments
- That which you are birthing in worship will be the leading edge of an evangelistic move in nations
- You will see your sons filling stadiums
- This move is going to gather pace
- Great favor is in front of you

STEP THREE:

Form a crafted prayer of declaration and thanksgiving from God's promises towards the recipient of these words.

Lord, thank You that You have intentionally invited me to take part in restoring the tribe of Asaph in the earth. You have graced me and equipped me for this call. Through me You will raise up a new sound in the earth. Thank You, Father, that You are giving me strategic wisdom and abundant provision for the nations. Thank You for the acceleration that is on my sons to become fathers and to birth that worship that will be the leading edge of evangelistic movements in nations. Father, You are faithful. You will do this.

ANSWER KEY: "PROCESSING CONDITIONS" PRACTICE

(Note: This is from Chapter 6.)

STEP ONE:

Identify conditional promises and command statements.

Sample Two

Last night I was praying for you, Dano, and the Lord told me that you are no longer going to be known as the town drunk. Because you've gone through a season of being foolish for God, and now you are going to confound the wise.

And yeah, a change in season—literally with your identity—there is a piece of your identity that you are leaving, and you are coming into a wise thing. I saw the Lord put a helmet on your head, and it said "wisdom" across the top of it. I feel like there is incredible strategic wisdom for the nations.

I feel like you are no longer going to be known for the foolishness—and I mean the foolishness we have when we follow God—but you are going to be known for your wisdom. So you have to take off that first season that the Lord had you in and put this one on. In Jesus' name. Amen.

Sample Three

Hundreds of thousands of dollars. Hundreds of thousands of dollars. Hundreds of thousands of dollars. Hundreds of thousands of dollars. The Lord says, too, that music companies and music stores are going to give you instruments. Music stores are going to give you instruments.

The Lord says that which you are birthing of worship in the earth will be the leading edge of an evangelistic move in the countries that you are working in. You will see your sons filling stadiums. Filling them. Filling them. Filling them. You are already starting to see it. Filling stadiums. For the Lord says it is going to increase because there is a quickening spirit upon you.

The Lord says of that which He has birthed in you, He says breathe on your sons even as Jesus breathed on His disciples and sent them. Breathe on your sons. Breathe on them. Because there is a quickening spirit. And the Lord says they don't have to know everything you know for there is a quickening spirit upon them because God is saying that they have to be accelerated. You see that in the spirit yourself. You see it in the spirit yourself.

For the Lord says there are more nations in His heart for you than what you are seeing right now. More nations in His heart for you. He is going to give you sons. I can see right now a dozen nations that God has given you sons in.

He says hundreds of thousands of dollars are going to come to you. He says ask Me. Ask Me. Ask Me for property; the answer is "yes." Ask Me for recording studios; the answer is "yes" because your sons will become fathers themselves in the anointing that God has given you.

The Lord says that He gives you a quickening spirit. The reason He wants you to breathe on your sons is so that they can go back and become fathers right quick because this is a move that is going to gather pace. It's going to gather pace. Gather pace. It is going to be like a rock rolling down a hill. It is going to go fast. It is going to go fast. So the Lord says great favor is in front of you. A huge wide open space is in front of you. Explore it!

STEP TWO:

Put the findings from each of the words you are processing into one table with the required action on one side and the promised outcome on the other.

Action	Outcome
Call forth a new sound	New songs will arise
Restore the Asaph prophetic order	Raise up worship leaders in the nations
Take off the first season and put on the new season of wisdom	Known for your wisdom
Continue what you are birthing in worship	Leading edge of evangelistic move in nations
Breathe on your sons	They will be accelerated
Breathe on your sons	They will become fathers quickly
Ask me for recording studios and property	The answer is "yes"

Step Three:

Create a MAP (Ministry Action Plan) from the conditions you highlighted.

I will call forth the new sound prophetically each time I'm in a nation.

I will look for Asaph's that carry the prophetic songs for nations.

I will embrace this new season of wisdom as I put aside the season of foolishness.

I will continue what I am birthing in worship in the earth.

I will breathe on my sons as Jesus breathed on His disciples.

I will ask of the Lord and keep on asking for the studios and properties He has promised and for the hundreds of thousands of dollars He has promised.

ANSWER KEY: "PROCESSING TIMES AND SEASONS" PRACTICE

(Note: This is from Chapter 7.)

STEP ONE:

Identify time and season indicators by drawing a triangle around any timing words.

Sample Two

Last night I was praying for you, Dano, and the Lord told me that you are no longer going to be known as the town drunk. Because you've gone through a season of being foolish for God, and now you are going to confound the wise.

And yeah, a change in season—literally with your identity—there is a piece of your identity that you are leaving, and you are coming into a wise thing. I saw the Lord put a helmet on your head, and it said "wisdom" across the top of it. I feel like there is incredible strategic wisdom for the nations.

I feel like you are no longer going to be known for the foolishness—and I mean the foolishness we have when we follow God—but you are going to be known for your wisdom. So you have to take off that first season that the Lord had you in and put this one on. In Jesus' name. Amen.

Sample Three

Hundreds of thousands of dollars. Hundreds of thousands of dollars. Hundreds of thousands of dollars. Hundreds of thousands of dollars. The Lord says, too, that music companies and music stores are going to give you instruments. Music stores are going to give you instruments.

The Lord says that which you are birthing of worship in the earth will be the leading edge of an evangelistic move in the countries that you are working in. You will see your sons filling stadiums. Filling them. Filling them. Filling them.

You are already starting to see it. Filling stadiums. For the Lord says it is going to increase because there is a quickening spirit upon you.

The Lord says of that which He has birthed in you, He says breathe on your sons even as Jesus breathed on His disciples and sent them. Breathe on your sons. Breathe on them. Because there is a quickening spirit. And the Lord says they don't have to know everything you know for there is a quickening spirit upon them because God is saying that they have to be accelerated. You see that in the spirit yourself. You see it in the spirit yourself.

For the Lord says there are more nations in His heart for you than what you are seeing right now. More nations in His heart for you. He is going to give you sons. I can see right now a dozen nations that God has given you sons in.

He says hundreds of thousands of dollars are going to come to you. He says ask Me. Ask Me. Ask Me for property; the answer is "yes." Ask Me for recording studios; the answer is "yes" because your sons will become fathers themselves in the anointing that God has given you.

The Lord says that He gives you a quickening spirit. The reason He wants you to breathe on your sons is so that they can go back and become fathers right quick because this is a move that is going to gather pace. It's going to gather pace. Gather pace. Gather pace. It is going to be like a rock rolling down a hill. It is going to go fast. It is going to go fast. So the Lord says great favor is in front of you. A huge wide open space is in front of you. Explore it!

STEP TWO:

Graph times and seasons by placing any promises related to specific timing words within their appropriate categories.

Times and Seasons Graph

Past	Present	Soon	Future
I used . . .		Will be used . . .	
The Lord has set you . . .		As the new song . . . When heaven . . . Then it will be . . .	

Past	Present	Soon	Future
No longer town drunk	Now confound the wise		
	change of season	coming into a wise thing	
No longer known for foolishness			Are going to be known for wisdom
	Already seeing (worship as leading edge of evangelism)		
	Sons have to be accelerated		
	More nations than you are seeing right now		
		move going to gather pace. Fast.	

STEP THREE:

Create a declaration of times and seasons.

- I have been . . .
- I am . . .
- I will soon . . .
- One day . . .

The following is an example of a declaration taken from a combination of times and seasons statements from Sample One. Add to the declaration using what you learned from the timing words in Sample Two and Three.

> God has already set me as an Asaph in the Body of Christ. I have been used and will continue to be used to restore the Levitical priesthood in the earth. As I call forth the new sound, heaven will respond, and then the realities of heaven will descend to the earth realm . . .

ANSWER KEY: "SPHERES OF INFLUENCE" PRACTICE

(Note: This is from Chapter 10.)

STEP ONE:

Look for any people, places, or special areas of interests. Place a dotted line under any indicators of sphere of influence.

Sample One

Lord, I bless Your minstrel prophet in the name of Jesus, that will be used—has been used—and will be used in an international manner to help restore the tribe of Asaph in the earth. I bless him in the name of the Lord.

We are all general practitioners, but God gives us specialty grace you see. And I just acknowledge that the Lord has set you into the Body as one of the Asaphs that raises up the prophetic Levitical priests to set them in divine order so as to call forth a new sound.

And as the new sound comes forth, heaven responds to the sound of earth. And when heaven responds to the sound of earth, heaven comes down and joins in the sound of earth. Then, it becomes not only our praises ascending but heaven has just descended into the earth realm.

So you are called as a culture creator, and an atmospheric changer to help restore the Asaph priesthood of prophetic order. In Jesus' name. Amen.

Would you say there were any location or geographic definers in this prophetic word? If so, what were the words that talked about a specific location?

Geographic sphere would be indicated by the words: international, in the earth,

Also, did you notice that this word is a promise for a specific interest group? The promises would not apply to everyone. What is the sociographic sphere or specific interest group that this prophetic word speaks to?

Sociographic sphere would be indicated by: "tribe of Asaph," "Levitical priesthood." These terms historically speak of worship leaders, singers, and musicians.

Check the other two sample words for people, places, and interest groups that might define a sphere of influence. See if Samples Two and Three point to the same or different spheres of influence than Sample One. Place a dotted line beneath any words that seem to assign sphere to a people, place, or interest.

Sample Two

Last night I was praying for you, Dano, and the Lord told me that you are no longer going to be known as the town drunk. Because you've gone through a season of being foolish for God, and now you are going to confound the wise.

And yeah, a change in season—literally with your identity—there is a piece of your identity that you are leaving, and you are coming into a wise thing. I saw the Lord put a helmet on your head, and it said "wisdom" across the top of it. I feel like there is incredible strategic wisdom for the nations.

I feel like you are no longer going to be known for the foolishness—and I mean the foolishness we have when we follow God—but you are going to be known for your wisdom. So you have to take off that first season that the Lord had you in and put this one on. In Jesus' name. Amen.

Sample Three

Hundreds of thousands of dollars. Hundreds of thousands of dollars. Hundreds of thousands of dollars. Hundreds of thousands of dollars. The Lord says, too, that music companies and music stores are going to give you instruments. Music stores are going to give you instruments.

The Lord says that which you are birthing of worship in the earth will be the leading edge of an evangelistic move in the countries that you are working in. You will see your sons filling stadiums. Filling them. Filling them. Filling them. You are already starting to see it. Filling stadiums. For the Lord says it is going to increase because there is a quickening spirit upon you.

The Lord says of that which He has birthed in you, He says breathe on your sons even as Jesus breathed on His disciples and sent them. Breathe on your sons. Breathe on them. Because there is a quickening spirit. And the Lord says they don't have to know everything you know for there is a quickening spirit upon them because God is saying that they have to be accelerated. You see that in the spirit yourself. You see it in the spirit yourself.

For the Lord says there are more nations in His heart for you than what you are seeing right now. More nations in His heart for you. He is going to give you sons. I can see right now a dozen nations that God has given you sons in.

He says hundreds of thousands of dollars are going to come to you. He says ask Me. Ask Me. Ask Me for property; the answer is "yes." Ask Me for recording studios; the answer is "yes" because your sons will become fathers themselves in the anointing that God has given you.

The Lord says that He gives you a quickening spirit. The reason He wants you to breathe on your sons is so that they can go back and become fathers right quick because this is a move that is going to gather pace. It's going to gather pace. Gather pace. It is going to be like a rock rolling down a hill. It is going to go fast. It is going to go fast. So the Lord says great favor is in front of you. A huge wide open space is in front of you. Explore it!

STEP TWO:

Bullet the information you underscored in the space provided below.

- tribe of Asaph
- in the earth
- worship

STEP THREE:

Categorize the information of people, places and interest groups into the three paragraphs below.

Geographic Sphere: "Where should I focus my efforts?"

Answer: In the nations of the earth.

Demographic Sphere: "Who should I be serving?"

Answer: No limit to demographic sphere, but there is an emphasis on spiritual sons.

Sociographic Sphere: "What am I best equipped to do?"

Answer: Raise up the new sound among worship leaders, singers, and musicians. Interact with music stores, music companies, and recording studios.

ANSWER KEY: "SYMBOLS, TYPES, AND METAPHORS" PRACTICE

(Note: This is from Chapter 12.)

STEP ONE:

Place an asterisk (*) by any word that might be a symbol, type, or metaphor.

Sample Two

Last night I was praying for you, Dano, and the Lord told me that you are no longer going to be known as the *town drunk. Because you've gone through a season of being foolish for God, and now you are going to confound the wise.

And yeah, a change in season—literally with your identity—there is a piece of your identity that you are leaving, and you are coming into a wise thing. I saw the Lord put a *helmet on your head, and it said "wisdom" across the top of it. I feel like there is incredible strategic wisdom for the nations.

I feel like you are no longer going to be known for the foolishness—and I mean the foolishness we have when we follow God—but you are going to be known for your wisdom. So you have to *take off that first season that the Lord had you in and *put this one on. In Jesus' name. Amen.

Sample Three

Hundreds of thousands of dollars. Hundreds of thousands of dollars. Hundreds of thousands of dollars. Hundreds of thousands of dollars. The Lord says, too, that music companies and music stores are going to give you instruments. Music stores are going to give you instruments.

The Lord says that which you are *birthing of worship in the earth will be the leading edge of an evangelistic move in the countries that you are working in. You will see your sons filling stadiums. Filling them. Filling them. Filling them.

You are already starting to see it. Filling stadiums. For the Lord says it is going to increase because there is a quickening spirit upon you.

The Lord says of that which He has *birthed in you, He says *breathe on your sons even as Jesus breathed on His disciples and sent them. Breathe on your sons. Breathe on them. Because there is a quickening spirit. And the Lord says they don't have to know everything you know for there is a quickening spirit upon them because God is saying that they have to be accelerated. You see that in the spirit yourself. You see it in the spirit yourself.

For the Lord says there are more nations in His heart for you than what you are seeing right now. More nations in His heart for you. He is going to give you *sons. I can see right now a dozen nations that God has given you sons in.

He says hundreds of thousands of dollars are going to come to you. He says ask Me. Ask Me. Ask Me for property; the answer is "yes." Ask Me for recording studios; the answer is "yes" because your sons will become fathers themselves in the anointing that God has given you.

The Lord says that He gives you a quickening spirit. The reason He wants you to breathe on your sons is so that they can go back and become fathers right quick because this is a move that is going to gather pace. It's going to gather pace. Gather pace. It is going to be *like a rock rolling down a hill. It is going to go fast. It is going to go fast. So the Lord says great favor is in front of you. A huge wide open space is in front of you. Explore it!

STEP TWO:

Make a list of the symbols, types, and metaphors you found.

- Levitical priests, Asaph priesthood
- nations, earth, countries, nations God has given sons in
- music companies, music stores
- Minstrel prophet
- Asaph
- General Practitioner
- Specialists
- Levitical Priests
- Culture Creators
- Take off current season
- Put on new season
- Birthing of worship
- sons
- breathe on your sons
- like a rock rolling down a hill

- Atmospheric Changers
- Town drunk
- Helmet of "wisdom"

STEP THREE:

Formulate questions for research, meditation, and prayer based on your list.

- What is a minstrel prophet?
- What do they do?
- How am I like one?
- Who was Asaph?
- How did he raise up the Levitical priesthood?
- How did he call forth a new sound?
- How does what he did relate to me?
- How does a general practitioner differ from a specialist?
- In what way am I a specialist?
- In what way am I a culture creator?
- Who are some culture creators I should study?
- How is culture created?
- What is an atmospheric changer?
- How is an atmosphere changed?
- What are some things that change atmospheres?
- How do these things relate to me?
- Why compare a helmet? What does a helmet do?
- Does the word "literal sons" mean? What would a symbolic son be?
- How is worship birthed?

About the Author

Dan McCollam travels internationally as a prophetic speaker and trainer. He strategizes with churches and individuals to create prophetic cultures in which everyone can hear God, activate and mobilize their prophetic words, and express their own unique prophetic diversity.

Dan has developed many resources that offer a fresh perspective on the prophetic, supernatural Kingdom life, biblical character, and spiritual gifting. He is well-known as a great friend of the Holy Spirit and one who carries and imparts wisdom, revelation, and breakthrough.

Dan serves on the teaching faculty of Bethel School of the Prophets and the Bethel School of Worship, in Redding, California. Along with his wife, Regina, Dan serves on the core leadership team at his home church, The Mission, in Vacaville, California, where he oversees a vibrant prophetic and worship community.

Sounds of the Nations

After serving as a worship leader for 20 years and releasing Kingdom worshipers locally, regionally, and globally on countless mission trips to nations around the world, Dan became troubled over the westernization of worship in the majority of churches in which he ministered. Indigenous sounds had often been labeled "sinful" by church leadership. Since the sounds of every tribe and nation are heard in heaven, becoming an agent in restoring the stolen authentic expressions of worship became a driving passion for Dan, and Sounds of the Nations was born.

As international director of Sounds of the Nations, Dan trains indigenous peoples to write and record worship songs using their own ethnic sounds, styles, languages, and instruments.

For more information about Sounds of the Nations, contact us by email: SOTNtraining@gmail.com.

Other books and resource materials by Dan McCollam

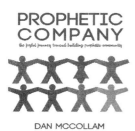

PROPHETIC COMPANY: We are living in an unprecedented resurgence of prophetic gifts and graces. Healthy expressions of the gift of prophecy most often emerge from those who have discovered the key of living in a true and vital connection with community. The pages of this book unearth biblical and historical foundations for the concept of a prophetic company while laying a path forward of definitions and structures valuable for building strong and robust prophetic communities.
(Book)

BASIC TRAINING FOR PROPHETIC ACTIVATION: This powerful book unearths several simple tools that will fan into flame the gift of God that is in you. It is full of practical insights where you will learn: the prophetic nature of a name; how your five senses can be activated by Holy Spirit to receive heavenly insight; how to bring people into the Kingdom with the gift of prophecy; how to process your own prophetic words for greater empowerment.
(Book)

SPIRITUAL GIFTS: What does passionately pursuing these gifts of the Spirit look like in everyday life? Author and teacher Dan McCollam encourages the red-hot burning pursuit of biblical Christianity as he instructs powerful and practical ways to explore, express, and pursue the spiritual gifts described in 1 Corinthians 12:7-11.
(Audio CD)

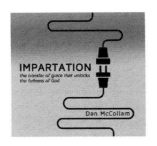

IMPARTATION through the laying on of hands is a fundamental teaching of the New Testament church. In this two-part series, Dan McCollam explores and activates five types of impartation: distributed, apprehended, residual, atmospheric, and relational. (Audio CD)

SPIRITUAL GIFTS: Based on 1 Corinthians 12:4-6, this teaching brings an understanding of the differing gifts, differing administrations and differing operations. Embracing the three-dimensional nature of spiritual gifts unlocks a greater freedom and operation of those gifts in the life of the believer. (Audio Set)

Volume One
Word of Wisdom
Word of Knowledge
Gift of Faith

Volume Two
Gifts of Healing
Working of Miracles
Gift of Prophecy

Volume Three
Gift of Discernment
Gift of Tongues
Interpretation of Tongues

Available at store.imissionchurch.com and Amazon.com.

MY SUPER POWERS is a series of children's books based on the nine gifts of the Holy Spirit mentioned in 1 Corinthians 12:8-9. Children don't receive a pint-sized Holy Spirit but all the fullness of God, the same as any adult. These stories are intended to show how children can operate in the gifts of the Spirit at an early age. (Book set)

All resources are available at:

store.imissionchurch.com

Digital resources available at:

SoundsoftheNations.com

Made in the USA
Columbia, SC
24 May 2019